Advance praise for
The Law of Attraction in Action

"Deanna explains in understandable terms how the Law of Attraction is worn in ordinary circumstances—like your most comfortable shoes. With purposeful willingness she shows how you can walk, in small achievable ways, to a place of transformation. This is a primer for those curious and new to the process and it is an engaging 'playbook' for practitioners who want to sharpen their game."

—Mary Anne Radmacher, author of
Lean Forward into Your Life

"It's an art to dream big dreams, and there's a science behind making those dreams come true. *The Law of Attraction in Action* explores both that art and that science in a powerful yet infinitely practical way. If you want to live the life of your dreams, this book is the perfect tour guide for that glorious adventure."

—Marcia Wieder, author of *Making Your Dreams Come True*
and *Dreams Are Whispers from the Soul*

"If you want to unlock the power of your destiny and attract the life you were born to live, you've come to the right place. Deanna artfully blends science with strategy and wisdom with wit in this brilliant guide to mastering the Law of Attraction. *The Law of Attraction in Action* is a powerhouse of insight, inspiration, and action for anyone ready to purposefully design their destiny."

—Peggy McColl, author of the *New York Times*
bestseller *Your Destiny Switch*

THE LAW OF
ATTRACTION
IN ACTION

A DOWN-TO-EARTH GUIDE TO TRANSFORMING YOUR LIFE
(NO MATTER WHERE YOU'RE STARTING FROM)

Deanna Davis, PhD

A Perigee Book

A PERIGEE BOOK
Published by the Penguin Group
Penguin Group (USA) Inc.
375 Hudson Street, New York, New York 10014, USA
Penguin Group (Canada), 90 Eglinton Avenue East, Suite 700, Toronto, Ontario M4P 2Y3, Canada
(a division of Pearson Penguin Canada Inc.)
Penguin Books Ltd., 80 Strand, London WC2R 0RL, England
Penguin Group Ireland, 25 St. Stephen's Green, Dublin 2, Ireland (a division of Penguin Books Ltd.)
Penguin Group (Australia), 250 Camberwell Road, Camberwell, Victoria 3124, Australia
(a division of Pearson Australia Group Pty. Ltd.)
Penguin Books India Pvt. Ltd., 11 Community Centre, Panchsheel Park, New Delhi—110 017, India
Penguin Group (NZ), 67 Apollo Drive, Rosedale, North Shore 0632, New Zealand
(a division of Pearson New Zealand Ltd.)
Penguin Books (South Africa) (Pty.) Ltd., 24 Sturdee Avenue, Rosebank, Johannesburg 2196, South Africa

Penguin Books Ltd., Registered Offices: 80 Strand, London WC2R 0RL, England

While the author has made every effort to provide accurate telephone numbers and Internet addresses at the time of publication, neither the publisher nor the author assumes any responsibility for errors, or for changes that occur after publication. Further, the publisher does not have any control over and does not assume any responsibility for author or third-party websites or their content.

Copyright © 2008 by Deanna Davis, PhD
Text design by Kristin del Rosario

First edition: August 2008

Library of Congress Cataloging-in-Publication Data

Davis, Deanna.
    The law of attraction in action : a down-to-earth guide to transforming your life (no matter where you're starting from) / Deanna Davis.— 1st ed.
        p. cm.
    Includes bibliographical references.
    ISBN 978-0-399-53434-8
    1. Success. I. Title.
    BF637.S8D355 2008
    158.1—dc22   2008011576

PRINTED IN THE UNITED STATES OF AMERICA

10 9 8 7 6 5 4 3 2 1

Most Perigee books are available at special quantity discounts for bulk purchases for sales promotions, premiums, fund-raising, or educational use. Special books, or book excerpts, can also be created to fit specific needs. For details, write: Special Markets, Penguin Group (USA) Inc., 375 Hudson Street, New York, New York 10014.

For G.G.—
you are the most exquisite and elegant example
of intentional action I've ever known.

And for my boys, the Three Cs:
Chad, Chase, and Carsten—
may your minds always be open,
your hearts always be full,
and your lives always be filled with wonder and adventure.

ACKNOWLEDGMENTS

Marian Lizzi and Cathy Hemming, if ever there were a dream team in the literary world, the two of you have earned the title. You are both clearly examples of women who went into the business for the right reasons and whose work changes the world. Marian, your expertise as an editor is only overshadowed by your gracious, warm nature and your contagious passion for what you do. Cathy, my super agent, your above-and-beyond style and authentic commitment to me and my work is positively inspiring. Thank you both for championing this project and for making it as important to you as it is to me. And my gratitude to the whole team at Perigee whose hard work made this book not only possible but also a pleasure to write.

Peggy McColl, I am grateful for your mentorship, your many contributions to our field, and for introducing me to Cathy. Mary Anne Radmacher, as always, your work, your warmth, and your wisdom make my creative and professional evolution truly magical.

My fondest appreciation to all of the wonderful researchers, practitioners, and teachers in the fields of the Law of Attraction, Positive Psychology, mind/body health, and neuroscience for your pioneering work to make this material meaningful and transformative for so many people. Special thanks to Jack Canfield and Bob Doyle for providing personal mentorship to me, and to Rhonda Byrne, all of the teachers in *The Secret*, and Esther and Jerry Hicks for launching a worldwide awareness of Law of Attraction principles.

A heartfelt thanks to all of my clients and audience members for sharing their questions and stories, and for helping me refine all of this material to make it accessible, meaningful, and transformative.

My mighty mastermind team, Betsy, Jen, Kerri, David, Matt, and Jodie—I am so grateful to have learned so much from and practiced these principles with all of you. You have been consummate educators, accountability partners, and examples of what really works.

Very special appreciation to Brett and Barbra for your friendship, which I will treasure for life, and for the soul-searching conversations that always lead me to want to explore more.

Kristie, Michelle, Alicia, Kay, Connie M., Brianna, Debbie, Kari, Lisa, Katie, and Susan (whew!), I'll never be able to thank you enough for your practical and emotional support while I gave birth to both Carsten and this book at the same time. It was quite the adventure and you were all the most supportive tour guides along that journey. Thanks for your friendship and love, the food (oh, yes, the food!), child care, garage reorganization, "nesting by proxy," and basically the sanity you afforded me during that time. (And thank you most of all for not challenging my use of the word *sanity*, since I know I may not have appeared so during those sleep-deprived months!).

Aunt Karen, you were my first mentor in learning about alternative and integrative health (and all things mindful), and Aunt Phyllis, you are a skilled and tireless literary (and life-affirming) cheerleader—thank you both for sharing your gifts. Along with my sisters, you are both examples of how Mom and Dad continue to be present in my life long after they moved on to new horizons. G.G., you are a role model to be reckoned with!

Amber, Rhee, Chad, and Malina, you are always so positive, supportive, and genuinely interested in all of my efforts, which makes it easy to continue to do what I love. Carsten, even without words, your smile inspires me daily.

And Michael, once again I am nearly speechless (a rarity, as you well know). I am so blessed to be graced by your friendship, your partnership, and your love. No one is more personally invested in my happiness and success than you are, and there is no one I would rather travel this marvelous journey of life with than you. God brought us together and provided our path, and you are the perfect companion to stroll down that path with peace and joy and purpose. I love you.

CONTENTS

PART ONE

HOW THE
LAW OF ATTRACTION
WORKS

Manifesting Meals, Mortgages, and Maui Manuscripts: My Story of the Law of Attraction in Action

The Olive Garden Experiment

It seems a little weird, I'll admit, but I started my Law of Attraction journey with a craving for endless soup, salad, and breadsticks. It's what I fondly refer to now as "The Olive Garden Experiment."

I had spent nearly a week in San Diego, away from my husband and three-year-old daughter, attending Jack Canfield's "Breakthrough to Success" workshop. It was there that I was introduced to the Law of Attraction (LOA), through a prerelease screening of the movie *The Secret*. I spent the entire night lying awake in bed, energized in one of those part-inspired, part-manic states (the kind you don't necessarily want to be in at 3 a.m.) musing about the possibility of readily attracting exactly what you want into your life. Was it really feasible to take the strain and strife out of creating the life of your dreams and replace it with a sense of ease and eagerness? If so, I was ready to sign on the dotted line.

I spent the next few days in a sleep-deprived stupor, playing little games here and there, attracting just the right resource in the bookstore or a serendipitous meeting with someone I'd wanted to talk with. I was jazzed about all the little bits of evidence I was collecting that the LOA works, so I doused my husband with enthusiasm during one of my calls home. My breathless tales left him intrigued, but hardly convinced. He absentmindedly affirmed my excitement with some version of "That sounds great, honey," while I'm sure he was simultaneously redirecting our toddler from impaling herself on something in the backyard. I sensed, though, that I'd swayed him past apathy to teeter on the brink of actual interest, so I suggested that maybe we could focus together on attracting something into our lives that we both really wanted. While he was decidedly *not* yet an LOA convert, he played along and we agreed to resume the discussion when I arrived home. I returned to the conference with a playful spirit, readily manifesting a healer for my aching back and a great connection for my new book. "Not a bad start," I thought.

As I continued my reflection, I figured there had to be a relationship between the LOA and my other areas of interest—Positive Psychology, mind/body health, and neuroscience. For years I'd been compiling studies and strategies that proved you could transform your life by changing how you think. Initially, these topics held a personal interest—I wanted to experience the most fulfilling and successful life I could, and used my educational pursuits (a master's degree focusing on health promotion and a PhD focusing on leadership and mind/body health) to explore the very best research on how to do that. In the words of my good friend, author Mary Anne Radmacher, I wanted to "live with intention." My quest led to the publication of my first book, not surprisingly named *Living With Intention*. That book, along with my practice as a professional speaker and a coach, helped me move forward in my goal of helping *others* transform their lives in meaningful ways, just as I had successfully done.

And now I had found another tool that seemed to fit right into the mix of everything I knew made a difference in people's lives. I had witnessed the powerful ways that people had changed their lives for the better—enriching relationships, enhancing professional and financial success, improving well-being, and experiencing renewed purpose, meaning, and joy in life—using strategies from Positive Psychology, mind/body health, and neuroscience. I started to believe that maybe the LOA simply provided another framework—and maybe a slightly different language—for expressing the concepts I'd been researching and following in these other areas for so many years.

So I left the conference to fly home and spent the entire trip brainstorming all the links that came to mind between the LOA and my areas of interest and expertise. By the time the plane touched down, my mind was again spinning with possibilities for sharing this life-changing information with as many people as I could. But first, I needed food. I'm a firm believer that one should not undertake changing the world (or even a lightbulb, for that matter) on an empty stomach. I immediately thought that nothing sounded better than an endless supply of soup, salad, and breadsticks. It seemed like an appropriate meal to begin helping people tap into the endless supply of possibilities that the LOA presents. I can rationalize almost anything. I thought to myself, "Olive Garden, here I come."

Then it hit me. My husband had been boycotting the Olive Garden for years, convinced that the restaurant (nestled as it is in the bustling metropolis of downtown Spokane, Washington) is seriously low on parking spots and painfully slow in service. It's true, he did always seem to repel convenient parking and attentive service, but I decided that this was because he had been attracting these outcomes because of his *bad Olive Garden mojo*, since I routinely had the exact opposite experience when I went with colleagues or friends. I always had stellar service and usually found the closest parking spot to the door. Thus, I surmised, I must have *good Olive Garden mojo.*

We even turned the Olive Garden into our own little inside joke for a few years there. I'd suggest going there every few months and he'd shake his head vigorously, saying something like, "Great idea . . . and why don't we chew on tinfoil for the rest of the night, too?" So, I'd go on my own, and each time I was there, I would ask the waitress or waiter to send a personalized note to my husband, which I gladly delivered. The notes would say something like, "Michael, please come back to the Olive Garden! It's not the same here without you!" and "From all of us here at the Olive Garden, please come see us again . . . we miss you!" I'd hand him each note, often punctuated with a smiley face or a series of exclamation points. He would read each one, try valiantly not to smile, roll his eyes, and toss the note into the trash. The collective efforts of many Olive Garden staff members and myself were not enough to make him budge, so I figured that maybe the LOA could. It was worth a try.

As my plane landed, I figured now would be as good a time as any to put the LOA to the test. I'd been gone for nearly a week from a clingy three-year-old who would with all certainty Velcro herself to me and emotionally punish me all evening for having temporarily abandoned her. My husband would, no doubt, be the slightest bit fatigued from having single-parented a precocious pre-schooler 24/7 for a week. And we would all be hungry, tired, and maybe just a bit moody. What an opportunity!

So as I was packing up my notes on the LOA, I focused in on the whole concept that it's all about *being very clear about what you desire,* and about *choosing a favorable energy state that will support bringing it to fruition.* I was ready. I got off the plane to a hearty welcome from my family and we chatted about the week as we headed toward the baggage claim. "I'm hungry," said my daughter, Malina. My husband nodded. "I am, too." I stepped up to the LOA platform like an Olympic athlete and dove into the minestrone with a 9.9 level of difficulty. "So am I," I said. "How about dinner at the Olive Garden?" Malina bounced around like a pinball, excited at the prospect of going out to dinner, and I shot a quick glance at my husband for his predictable response. He rolled his eyes, shook his head slightly, and owing to sheer exhaustion, I'm sure, whispered an exasperated "Fine," accompanied by the requisite pout.

"LOA, one point," I thought. We headed to the car and chatted back and forth about the conference, their week, the LOA, and the like. In the lull between conversations I'd focus all my mental energy on creating a great dining experience—light traffic downtown, convenient parking, no line at the restaurant, a fabulous server, and an excellent meal. We reached downtown with no real traffic to contend with, and headed toward the restaurant. We slipped right into one of the best parking spots in the garage and headed to the entrance. "Two more points for the LOA," I mused. As we walked up to the restaurant, I could see people crowded outside the door. From the corner of my eye I could see my husband tense up, again roll his eyes, and shake his head with an indignant "I knew it." He was ready, willing, and able to dish up a serious complaint or two.

I gently and lovingly ignored him as I strolled up to the hostess. "Three for dinner, please," I said, glancing at the mass of people standing around waiting for their feeding frenzy to commence. Much to my surprise, she grabbed three menus and said, "Right this way!" It was like the seas parting as she escorted us to our table. I could have sworn I even heard a choir of angels singing. "The LOA's really racking up the points now. Right on," I thought. No sooner had we arrived at the table than a server appeared with a hefty wine jug in hand (which may actually have been the thing that won Michael over, since I sensed he had to refrain from hugging the young man). The waiter proceeded to fill our glasses and take our orders.

The evening went on with an almost eerie display of ease and good fortune—a good meal, great service, a startlingly contented child, and some inspiring conversation about the power of the LOA. When we concluded our evening out, my mind was even fuller than my belly and Michael quietly gave in to the notion that there really is something to the LOA. "Okay, I'm convinced," he said. "Of what?" I asked. "Well," he said, "if this Law of Attraction thing can work on the Olive Garden after all these years, I guess it can probably work on just about anything." And thus began our journey.

Little House on the Prairie

I brought Michael up to speed on all the LOA principles and we both dove into the study and practice of applying it to our lives. We decided to partner together for a mutual LOA experiment or two, starting with the intent to sell our current home and find the ideal land to build a new one. Our home had been on the market for over six months with little to no interest, since the winters where we live are gorgeous but can be treacherously snowy at times. The major drawback to our home was an alarmingly steep driveway, complete with matching staircase leading to the front door. While appropriate for mountain goats, these features were less appealing to humans, making the trek into our home daunting in good weather and dangerous in bad. So if the driveway of a thousand nightmares didn't effectively morph curb appeal into curb repel, the staircase certainly did. As such, we had a slew of "drive-bys" that resulted in people gunning it past our home and haphazardly fishtailing their way toward the sanity of one-floor ranchers in the neighborhood. We did have one buyer, a California resident unfamiliar with our winter blunderland, who had put an offer contingent on the sale of his home. His home, though (and subsequently ours), remained on the market, untouched for months.

Our impatience mounted, and we prepared to pull the house off the market for a while, if for no other reason than to enjoy a reprieve from the impossible task of keeping our home clean for more than seven minutes at a time. The reality of having a three-year-old in the house, combined with a penchant for housekeeping only slightly more robust than enduring multiple root canals while listening to a symphony of nails on a chalkboard, had made keeping our home "showable" just about as likely as keeping my diet "chocolate free." Not only laughable, but nearly impossible (and let's be honest, for the most part undesirable). So we had given ourselves a time line, and decided that if we didn't have a valid sale within two weeks, we would pull the house off the market and live for a little while in cluttered but relaxed bliss until we experienced some tidiness revelation.

After learning about the LOA, though, we realized that we had been mistakenly focused on successfully *not* selling our home so that we could take it *off* the market, rather than on *selling* our home so that it would no longer be *on* the market. It was more than just semantics—this seemingly insignificant choice of wording and focus made all the difference in the world. We decided to focus our intention on the prospect of securing the *ideal* buyer at the *ideal* price within our two-week time frame. We certainly had nothing to lose and everything to gain, so we set about visualizing our desired outcome and choosing a favorable emotional state about our prospects.

Just one day later I received a call from my realtor. Our buyer in California had received a solid, noncontingent offer on his home.

They were still processing paperwork but everything appeared as though his sale—and as a result, ours—was going to go through just fine. We were ecstatic, starting to truly believe that there definitely is *something* to this LOA phenomenon.

The sale moved forward without a hitch and we turned our attention toward the purchase of land for our new home. Owing to the slow sale of our house, we previously had lost our option on two different parcels of land that we thought were perfect for us, so we had stopped actively looking for a while. When we started looking again, we learned that there was simply nothing on the market even close to what we were looking for. So we decided to just keep envisioning all the aspects of our perfect parcel and have faith that we would find it in good time. Within just a couple of days of selling our home and focusing on finding the ideal new land, we stumbled across an unbelievable parcel in exactly the location and school district we wanted. It sat on a prairie with glorious views on all sides. And it just happened to be the lowest-priced lot in a high-demand area. We submitted an offer that day and secured the lot, which was far more "perfect" than anything we had previously seen or placed an offer on.

We began planning for the home itself—our "little house on the prairie"—and the LOA magic continued. We unexpectedly linked up with an extremely talented architect, who designed our custom home for a fraction of the anticipated cost. Our builder, a good friend, just happened to be perfectly poised between jobs to build our home for us. We were referred to a great lender, who not only approved our loan in record time but also fast-tracked our closing so that we could leave on vacation, comfortable that the land and home were ours. Things were good. And then came the real test.

We were within a week of closing on our new home and land when a huge payment came due for a substantial investment in our business. It was a larger sum of money than we had ever spent, and the need for it came at *exactly* the moment when cash flow had slowed between projects and we were getting ready to close on our new home. We didn't want to jeopardize our loan closing by maxing out our credit, even if it was only for a short time. We didn't have a ready solution to make the payment and we weren't sure how to resolve this significant need. And at the same time, I was faced with a massive influx of deliverables for the new business venture and felt entirely overwhelmed. Time for a different approach to the situation.

I had been intrigued by an exercise I learned about in a wonderful book called *Ask and It Is Given*, by Esther Hicks, so I thought I'd give it a try. The exercise was called the Place Mat process, a strategy you can use when you are feeling overwhelmed and overburdened or unsure of how you will be able to manage everything you need to do. The instructions were simple: Take out a large sheet of paper (like a place mat), and on one side list all the things that you are committed to doing that day—the top tasks that you most want and need to do that day. On the other side of the paper, list all the things you are asking the Universe to take care of for you.

Now, I'll admit that this process did lean a bit toward the "woo-woo" side of things for me. I mean, last time I checked, the Universe was not on my payroll. And as I recalled, the Universe had never left me an unexpected note on the kitchen counter saying, "Don't worry about the so-and-so . . . I've taken care of it." But I was pretty convinced that this LOA thing was working, and my own anxious searches for a solution weren't, so I figured it was worth a try. After all, since I didn't have the time . . . or the solutions . . . for a number of things on my list, it seemed logical that if I wasn't going to be able to accomplish it all anyway, why not take it off my list and focus on what I *could* do?

I started my list, and before long, I realized that I still had twenty things on my side of the paper and the Universe was accountable only for the laundry and cleaning the kitchen. Truth be told, I didn't know how the Universe was going to accomplish even those two things, but I certainly knew that I didn't have the time (much less the interest!) to take care of them myself. As I reflected, I also didn't have time for a lot of the other things on my list, so I started getting ruthless.

I moved as much as I possibly could to the Universe's side, keeping only what I knew *must* be done *today* and *by me*. This actually started feeling kind of good! Then I got to the item on the list that read, "Pay huge investment bill for the business this week." I knew without a doubt that I didn't have the money to pay this bill and didn't anticipate sufficient cash flow for several weeks. Now, I wasn't convinced that the Universe was going to cosign a loan for me or pawn some of its tools to pay my bills, but since I didn't see a way to resolve the issue, I figured it needed to go on the Universe's list so that I would be able to focus on what I *did* have control over that day.

I finished the list and got to work on my side of the universal bargain. Things hummed right along—I was marking things off my list left and right. Then, something cool started to happen. Many of the things on the Universe's side started getting done, even though I had consciously decided to focus on other things. People I needed to talk with would unexpectedly call, a deadline would be moved, or someone would offer help. It felt a little eerie, but I wasn't complaining. I just hummed the theme from *The Twilight Zone* and kept on cruising. In fact, I finished most of my tasks so quickly and efficiently, that I actually had time and energy to complete a few of the Universe's tasks as an act of goodwill. I would have given the Universe even more credit for the progress, but I felt justified in withholding some praise to compensate for personally having to load the dishwasher.

At the end of the day, there was a lot more done on both my list and the Universe's list than I would have thought possible. But a quick review reminded me that "pay huge investment bill" was still there on the list like a flashing neon sign. I started to feel a twinge of anxiety but quickly realized that I had committed to *focusing on the result I wanted*—sanity and efficiency today, and the huge bill paid somehow within the week. Again, since I didn't have an immediate resolution, I decided to release it for now and see what tomorrow would bring. And tomorrow brought an interesting turn of events.

Less than twenty-four hours later, I received an unexpected call from my lender. "I have good news," she said. "Your appraisal came in $40,000 over your purchase price for your home. That means you have built-in equity. Do you want to use that equity toward your down payment?" I was stunned. One day ago I had no idea how I was going to pay for this huge, unwieldy bill, and still have enough cash—and clear credit—for a smooth and uneventful closing on the house. Now I had access to far more financial resources than I needed. The down payment and financing were intact and I had all I needed to pay the mega-business-investment-bill. I was elated. I looked at the list, with so many things crossed off my side (from my own efforts) and from the Universe's side (from a combination of factors, most of which I didn't consciously influence) and saw proof that the LOA not only works . . . but sometimes works wonders.

We are now joyfully living in our little house on the prairie, an outcome we attribute to the LOA at its finest.

Manifesting Maui and Manuscripts

There was one final event that forever imprinted the power of the LOA on our hearts and minds—and on this book. We had just returned from a trip to Maui, our first in several years for a variety of reasons. We were rested and ready to get back into the swing of things, although a bit melancholy about making the transition from paradise to paperwork and from relaxation to real work. Within a couple of days of our return, my in-box produced a gorgeous brochure for the Maui Writer's Conference, an event I had long dreamed of attending. I leafed through it, still able to smell the tropical air and feel the warmth on my skin, and thought, "Wouldn't it be great to be able to attend this event someday?" I looked at the dates and realized that they were just a little over two months away. I started to tell myself that there was certainly no way it could happen this year, since we had just returned from our vacation there. How selfish (or possible) would it be to go back within just a couple of months? I stopped myself in my tracks. "Why not take a minute to dream?" I thought. "It doesn't hurt anything and would give me a temporary reprieve from slogging through the bottomless abyss of my in-box."

So I imagined what it would be like to actually board that plane in late August and head back to paradise, this time to focus on publishing my new book. I leafed through the brochure and highlighted all the names of the presenters I wanted to see. I recalled the location of the hotel in Wailea, just minutes from our favorite beach on the island. I pictured myself immersed in the energy and creativity of other writers, and walking away from the conference with a publishing deal for my new book on—you guessed it— the Law of Attraction. It was a heavenly little bliss break and I started feeling excited about the possibility, knowing that someday I would, indeed, be there—even if it wasn't for this year's conference.

Later that day, I mentioned the conference to my husband and shared the brochure with him. His eyes lit up for the moment at the prospect of returning to what we have come to know as our "second home." He was gung ho at the thought of going back, and we talked about the fact that it would be great to focus on planning that trip for the following year. "Wouldn't it be better, though, to go this year?" we said at the same time. We both agreed that it would. It felt a little decadent, though, and the reality of what it takes in terms of money and business logistics to make that trip made us pause. "Do you think it's too much to imagine going this year?" he asked. I admitted I'd thought the same thing, but then corrected myself and posed to him, "We've been seeing all sorts of evidence that this LOA stuff really works, so why don't we just focus on what we really want—to go to the conference *this year*, have a great time, and secure a publishing deal—and then sit back and see what happens? If we're not meant to go this year, then we'll start planning early for next year." We agreed we'd do just that and set up a playful strategy to focus on our desire to go. We started a game of looking for any "signs" that would tell us it was possible.

About an hour later, we were on the way to take our daughter to a movie, still excitedly chatting about Maui. A bumper sticker on the relic of a car in front of us stopped us both midsentence. It simply said, "Live Aloha." Now we live in Spokane, Washington, which is about as far from a model of Polynesian culture as you can get. And in our combined sixty years of living in that community, neither of us had ever seen a bumper sticker referencing anything having to do with Hawaii or Aloha. We looked at each other and in nearly the same breath said, "Well, we asked for signs and there's the first!" We continued our conversation about the potential trip with even more joy and animation than before.

We got to the theater, purchased our tickets, and headed to the concession stand for our standard movie provisions. Midtransaction, Michael turned to me and said, "Do you hear that?" I had to strain to hear the music over the crowd behind us but in a moment it was clear as a bell . . . the voice of our favorite Hawaiian artist, Israel Kamakawiwo'ole (Iz), singing his enchanting version of "Over the Rainbow." We looked at each other and smiled an incredulous smile. "Sign number two," I said.

The next day we were at the office working on some strategic planning. As we talked about our upcoming projects for the business, the subject of my new book came up, and again, so did the idea of going to Maui to help move its publishing prospects forward. We chuckled at the funny little signs we'd been seeing, and commented on how fun it was to just be creatively focusing on the *possibility* of manifesting this goal. We headed over to the coffee shop for a quick break. When we walked in, the first thing that jumped out at us was a display touting "our new featured product." There, in all their tropical glory, were rows and rows of Maui Potato Chips. We looked at each other and laughed, if nothing else, at the sheer entertainment value of yet another quirky bit of serendipity.

We were starting to feel such great energy around our little experiment that we decided we needed to seek out more definitive— and productive—signs that we were meant to go. I mean, bumper stickers and pop songs and potato chips are all nice, and they were yielding great cocktail party stories, no doubt, but these things certainly don't finance a trip to paradise. Practicality started taking over and we opened ourselves up to receiving *monetary* signs that the trip might be possible. (Smart move, don't you think?)

We headed back to the office and got back to work. An hour or so later, Michael came out of his office and said, "You won't believe what I found. I was playing around looking at travel packages around the time of the conference and I ran across the most amazing deal online." Sure enough, he had found a package for airfare and lodging for a little over 50 percent of our usual travel expense to Maui. We'd never seen such an outstanding travel deal.

I was stunned. Then intrigued. Then energized. "Hmmm . . . that's an interesting financial sign. Let's see if we might be able to attach that to a practical sign . . . one that actually involves *coming up with the money to get us there*." On we went, talking almost non-stop for the next twenty-four hours about our little adventure.

The next day we headed to one of my speaking engagements. It was a bit of a drive, so we spent our time in the car strategizing about how we might arrange the finances and business demands to get to Maui. It was really starting to look possible, to our surprise and delight, so we got more specific about what could transpire between now and then to make it happen. We arrived at my event in great spirits, and had a wonderful time with the attendees. I signed books and chatted with participants before we packed up to head home. When our assistant processed the receipts for the event, we were astonished. Not only did we have a fabulous time and meet some truly inspiring people, but we had brought in the highest gross receipts for any event I had spoken at. A final count of our earnings was almost *exactly* the amount of the travel bargain package Michael had uncovered online. We opted to take that as the sign that perhaps we were, indeed, meant to go. And with a bit more logistical work and strategic planning, we landed in Maui the day before the conference was scheduled to start, just two months after we had departed and said to ourselves, "Let's get back here sooner than later."

It doesn't stop there, though. The other part of what we wanted to manifest in Maui was a publishing contract for my new book. I envisioned this as the ultimate outcome of my time there, though I didn't exactly know how it would come to pass. I just set about being engaged and attentive, ready to learn everything I could while I was there. After poring over the bio and picture for every single editor and agent in attendance at the conference, I set up meetings with two agents and two editors. In all honesty, I focused less on their credentials and more on the "feel" of who they were, what *they* were passionate about, and whether I felt we would work well together on this project that *I* was so passionate about.

Indeed, each meeting was positive and energizing, and all four of them asked for the proposal for my book. I felt like these were early wins, but also knew the volume of writers they met with and the very small number of proposals they actually accepted. Still, though, I felt hopeful. I left the conference full of ideas and creativity, and with a newfound confidence that my book would find the perfect path to its audience. I took a moment to focus on gratitude and appreciation before I sent each proposal out, certain that the project would land with just the right person at just the right time. I detached myself from any specific outcome and set about all my other projects.

Months went by while I focused on cultivating uncommon patience (something new for me). As I worked on the manuscript, the content was shaping up exactly as I wanted it to, and the project was coming along beautifully. Then, out of the blue, on a Friday afternoon, it happened. I was teaching a day-long work-shop, which typically means that I do not check email or voice mail so that I won't be distracted. Something moved me to take a quick email break at lunchtime, and to my astonishment, the very top email on the list, sent only minutes before I logged on, was from Marian, who later became my editor. She loved the proposal and wanted to discuss taking it on. We talked about the project and she said she'd discuss it with her colleagues and get back to me.

Several weeks later, I woke from a dream with a rush of adrena-line. In my dream, I had just opened up my email in a rather dis-tracted way and the very top email was another one from Marian. I woke from the dream before I had a chance to read it, but I really didn't need to finish it because just six hours later, the top email in my box was from Marian, with a gracious note and solid offer for my new book—which you now hold in your hands. I was elated and overjoyed and . . . well, convinced beyond a shadow of a doubt . . . that the LOA does, indeed, work. Sometimes it's playful, sometimes a bit creative in its execution, but always exquisitely effective in delivering on desires when you allow it to, whether those desires are a meal, a mortgage, or a manuscript in Maui.

But It's Not All About Me

The reason I share these stories is simply to illustrate the evolution of my experience in embracing the LOA, and how that journey convinced me that if its principles can transform *my* life, they can do the same for *others*, including *you*. Throughout the book, you will also hear examples and stories from others who have used the LOA strategies to attract everything from a chai latte to an ideal partner and from a lost dog to weight loss (and everything in between). These are all *real* stories of *real* people who have influenced their life outcomes on so many levels—how they *think*, what they *decide*, and how they *act*. These tales are meant to illustrate that the LOA is as much about enjoying the *journey* toward what you desire as it is about reaching the *destination*. They show that the LOA is about maintaining a playful attitude and a learning mind, combined with an enduring sense of possibility and promise.

The examples of how others have customized LOA principles in ways that work for them are just a part of the equation. You will also find a wide array of key concepts and practical strategies that are steeped in science and proven in practice to help you design— and live—the life of your dreams. You'll learn that benefiting from the LOA is as much a matter of how you *think* as it is about what you *do*. It's as much about what you put *into* your mind as it is about what you *release* from it. And it's about feeling a sense of ease instead of urgency, eagerness instead of impatience, and flow instead of frenzy. It's about using all the creative, customized ways to put the Law of Attraction in Action in *your* life. Here's to taking that first step!

(*The LOA is as much a matter of how you think as it is about what you do.*)

CHAPTER ONE

Getting Past Groovy:
The Real Person's Guide
to the Law of Attraction

The Law of Attraction Defined

I'm assuming that if you've found your way to this book, you probably already know the basics about what the Law of Attraction *is* and simply want to learn more about how it *works* and how to make it work for *you*. If you are new to the LOA, an array of outstanding books, audios, and movies can introduce you to the concept in more depth (see "Resources" at the end of the book for a comprehensive list). The information presented here is designed to help you translate what you know into action—and results—in your life. Just to be sure we're all on the same page, though, we'll begin with a quick refresher course on basic concepts and terminology we'll be using as we explore the power of the LOA together.

You've probably heard a variety of descriptions and definitions of the LOA, including "Like attracts like," "You get what you think about," "Your thoughts determine your destiny," and "What you think about, you bring about." These are pretty standard ways of describing the notion that *how* and *where* you choose to direct your energy and focus will determine both the quality of your life *experiences* and the quality of your *outcomes*, both good and bad, positive and negative.

You see examples everywhere of the LOA in Action. You've heard tales of someone who focuses all her energy on the ways that she is a victim in her marriage and her friendships and her job, and how she miraculously continues to draw to her that very experience of being a victim over and over again. Likewise, someone who directs his attention toward how awful his financial situation is, how it's always been this way, and how everything he tries to do to improve it fails, predictably experiences those same outcomes in his finances. People who complain most about how sick and tired, overwhelmed and overworked, underappreciated and underpaid they are all seem to perpetually create those experiences for themselves. These results aren't just a matter of taking a misery pill, though, or tuning to the "bad karma" station of your crystal ball. These outcomes are the result of *ingrained patterns of thinking, believing, and behaving that produce undesirable life outcomes.*

On the other end of the spectrum, when people focus on what they *do* want to experience, have, or achieve, they seem to bring more of that into their lives. The person who *expects* to find fulfilling work that sustains a desired way of life tends to find it. The person who *anticipates* creating a satisfying marriage or enjoyable parenting experience seems to have much greater likelihood of doing so. And the person who *thinks and acts* in ways that support a vibrant vision for a business or charitable venture often reaches that goal, even in the face of inevitable challenges or setbacks. These are the positive results of the LOA. Again, though, these outcomes aren't a matter of hot-wiring some magic wand or sprinkling fairy dust on everything in sight—on the contrary, they are the result of *making conscious choices about how you think, what you focus on, and how you take action in your life.*

*The positive results of the LOA are the result of making
consapius choices about how you think, what you focus on,
and how you take action in your life.*

The LOA is *not* all just a matter of acting like Pollyanna on steroids. There's more to it than "If you think it, it will come." It's not just about *hoping* for the best or *anticipating* the best or even *expecting* the best (although what harm can that do?). It's also about *knowing with certainty* that when your idea of "the best" doesn't happen according to your particular plan or time line or schema, that you not only can *handle* it, but can *thrive* in that circumstance. This comes from the intrinsic knowledge and full conviction that you can learn, evolve, or transcend from this experience to realize something even better or more meaningful.

As I see it, the real beauty of the LOA is that it's strongly related to widely accepted and well-researched practices in a variety of fields of study. That body of research proves that changing your *perspective*, your *practices*, and taking *purposeful action* toward what you desire will yield lasting change for the better in your life. That's why this book is all about putting the Law of Attraction in *Action*. Before we get to that, though, it's helpful to address some of the "groovier" aspects of the LOA.

Dr. Groovy Gets It

I was sitting across from one of my favorite clients, the most down-to-earth and at the same time "big-thinker" physician I've ever known. We were discussing the principles of the LOA—he had just started learning more about it—and talking about how it applied to life, love, work, and just about everything. He was conceptually on board with the principles and felt that "there is definitely something to this," but there was one thing that was troubling him about the LOA. "Don't you think it's all just a little bit . . . *groovy?*" he said, objectively and unapologetically. I had the same concern myself, instead choosing to label some of the more metaphysical LOA premises and practices as "kind of woo-woo," and I told him so. Because the evidence seemed so compelling, though, we decided to explore these aspects a bit more.

He went on to share that most of the resources we'd turned to in our early work together on the LOA dealt with the concept in mostly metaphysical terms, sprinkled with random references to quantum physics that added an air of credibility. He had nothing against these books and videos and, on the contrary, really resonated with the content and the philosophical principles, just as I did. But when he started to peel back the layers, the "science geek" in him (and in me, to be honest) wanted something more—a more solid foundation for the principles that seemed to be pretty much aligned with common sense but presented in a way that felt a little too much like consulting a Magic 8-Ball for life guidance.

His comments are shared by others, too. In fact, one of the most common questions or criticisms I hear about the LOA when I speak to groups or work one-on-one with clients is the idea that "all you have to do is sit around thinking good thoughts and the Universe, like a genie, will serve up your every whim on a silver platter." Last time I checked, though, I didn't have a genie on staff, nor had I been informed that a distant relative had written the granting of my every wish into her will (though I admit that would be a lovely gesture). What I *have* experienced, thankfully, is that through a combination of *choosing my emotional state, setting a clear intention for what I desire, and taking inspired actions,* I can readily transport myself into the "flow" of experiencing, achieving, and attracting what I want to have in my life with relative ease. And I have witnessed countless others do the same.

I told Dr. Groovy that I'd been taking my study of the LOA to a deeper level. I had been integrating findings from a variety of fields that I felt supported the principles I intuitively knew to be true about the LOA from my own experience. Then, I expanded on that knowledge with objective observations of the LOA's positive impact on my own life and on the lives of others. He was intrigued and ready to explore more of these concepts, and that's when the pieces of the puzzle started to come together.

I started weaving findings from the fields of quantum physics, Positive Psychology, neuroscience, and mind/body health into my understanding of the LOA, and patterns started to emerge. The resistance I had felt to some of the more metaphysical interpretations of the LOA (which sometimes felt as if they were distilled down to wishful thinking and serendipity) started to fade. In their place, the more "logical" associations with science and practice rounded out my understanding so that it felt a lot easier to share the concepts with people who really wanted to embrace the LOA but were put off by what I now started referring to as "the groovy factor." I began to realize that there are predictable ways that people *think* and *act* that ultimately impact their likelihood of manifesting what they want. In a sense, it's a simple prescription: "When you change your mind, you change your behaviors, and change your life."

There are predictable ways that people think and act that ultimately impact their likelihood of manifesting what they want.

That's the Spirit

Given my leaning toward research-based and practice-tested elements of the LOA, the perpetual question I'm faced with about my interpretation is, "Where's spirituality in all of this?" In fact, many of the most prominent books, videos, and speakers on the subject of the LOA focus extensively, if not exclusively, on the notion that "something bigger than us" is responsible for all aspects of its functioning, whether you label that "bigger something" as God, Source, the Universe, a Higher Power, the energy field, or any number of other names. My take on this is simple. While I personally *do* believe that there's a "bigger force" out there than ourselves, and I believe that it creates the fabric of possibility and opportunity that I drape myself in every day, I also believe that we all have highly individual and unique ways of interpreting and practicing our spiritual beliefs. Likewise, I believe that we all have unique ways of thinking and behaving that yield results in our lives. The combination of those things is what makes the LOA itself, and every individual's experience with it, so powerful.

The principles I'll be talking about here are based in the realm of science and strategy, with a healthy dose of good humor and how-to. Your role is to explore these notions, determine which ones speak to you the most, and evaluate how they fit into your own spiritual practice. That makes the whole shebang not only more *personalized* (which is one of the main benefits of the LOA, if you ask me), but also more *meaningful* and more *powerful.* I've worked with people of all faiths who have used these principles to their benefit, and who have integrated the practices into their own belief structures, whether they consider themselves Christians or Buddhists, metaphysical or evangelical, Jewish or New Thought, or engage in any other practice. In fact, I've worked with a number of people who began their study of the LOA with an agnostic or atheistic stance, who arrived at a clear and profound sense that there is, indeed, "something bigger" than ourselves, even if they weren't able to describe what that is.

It all boils down to what makes sense to *you* and the decision *you* make to weave new information into your existing belief structure and practice, or to evolve your spiritual beliefs in a way that feels right to you. I leave the spirituality decisions up to you and focus instead here on the *science* and *strategy* of the LOA.

Science and Strategy

The science and strategy of the LOA bridge compelling research findings with effective practices that create real change. My intent here is *not* to present in-depth analyses and statistical findings of every study related to the LOA. You can rest easily now. On the contrary, it's really just a matter of offering a sampling of the research from a variety of disciplines that I believe create a better understanding of how the LOA works. The following is a quick overview of those different disciplines, but you'll find examples of the research from these fields throughout the rest of the book, mostly as a tool to show that the LOA is more than just wishful thinking—its core concepts are aligned with reputable research from well-known fields. The four primary arenas I'll be referring to are quantum physics, Positive Psychology, mind/body health, and neuroscience. The following section provides a quick overview of how they are related to the LOA.

Quantum Physics. When people talk about the "science" behind the LOA, the most commonly referenced field of study is quantum physics, with a particular focus on the idea that "everything is energy," and that you can influence that energy with intentional thought. Some interpret this idea to mean not only that everything is *connected* at the energy level, but also that our thoughts and energy can influence *more than just our own experience*—they can influence *the field of energetic connections among people and circumstances as well.*

There are a few principles from quantum physics that are most often referenced when discussing the LOA. The first is that everything is energy—discrete little packets of energy that form what we perceive as reality, whether you're talking about your nose, your bathroom sink, or your thoughts—and that this energy vibrates at a certain "frequency" that gives each item its unique characteristics. The second is that we can influence that energy not only by the *actions* we take, but also by the *thoughts* we think and the ways that we *interact* with others and the world. It's not just about applying *physical* force to move energy; it's just as much about directing *mental* focus to influence that energy. The third is that quantum physics includes the concept of what is called the "observer effect," meaning that the simple act of consciously observing something changes its very nature, so everything that we look at, think about, or interact with is changed in some way simply because we observed it. Basically, we shape our reality by participating in it.

These are powerful concepts that are integral to understanding the LOA, but quantum physics isn't the only area of study associated with the LOA. In order to explore the research-based foundation for how and why the LOA works, it's helpful to look at the other disciplines associated with it. I tend to focus on several areas of study that I believe contribute the richest perspective to both an understanding of *why* the LOA works and to illustrating *how* it can work for you through the application of proven strategies. The disciplines I rely on when I teach these principles are Positive Psychology, mind/body health, and neuroscience.

Positive Psychology. To begin with, the Positive Psychology movement focuses on emotional *wellness* rather than emotional *illness*. It spans a variety of areas of study that stress strengths rather than weaknesses and assets rather than deficits. It asks important questions, such as "What makes people resilient?" "What contributes to quality of life?" and "What are the characteristics of peak life experience?" The study of Positive Psychology covers a wide range of characteristics of happy, satisfied people including (but not limited to) optimism, hope, resiliency, peak experience, social connection, forgiveness, and the identification and cultivation of our unique strengths. Decades of studies in the field have shown that these practices yield remarkable impacts on health, productivity, success, and fulfillment, among other things.

Contrary to some people's views that the term "positive" in Positive Psychology translates to "irrational and irritatingly upbeat," it's really more about adopting *constructive* ways of thinking and acting that benefit all aspects of your life. Thankfully for you and those around you, you don't just sit around singing "If You're Happy and You Know It" to benefit from Positive Psychology principles. Rather, you choose a mind-set that promotes genuine happiness and quality of life while focusing your thoughts in ways that allow you to navigate life's inevitable ups and downs with grace and purpose. Positive Psychology provides the foundation for strategies like optimism and gratitude, which are central to the successful practice of the LOA.

Positive Psychology is about adopting constructive ways of thinking and acting that benefit all aspects of your life.

Mind/Body Health. Mind/body health is a related field of study that, according to the National Institutes of Health, examines how the brain, mind, body, and behavior impact health. It's as concerned with the impact of emotional, mental, social, spiritual, and behavioral factors as it is about traditional measures of physical wellness. Mind/body health encompasses a variety of practices that impact well-being in body, mind, and spirit, such as meditation, relaxation, guided imagery, spiritual practices, yoga, and cognitive-behavioral therapy, among others. Hundreds of research studies have shown that the mind and body are linked in such a way that it is nearly impossible to determine where one ends and the other begins.

You are exposed to mind/body health concepts when you hear the common phrase, "If you go there in the mind, you'll go there in the body." It's part of mind/body health when people talk about the "placebo effect," where a treatment contains no active ingredients (commonly referred to as a "sugar pill") but has the same beneficial effects as an active treatment in reducing pain, discomfort, disorder, or disease simply because the patient *believes* it will work. Experiences like these illustrate the power of the mind to literally change or heal the body. And when you "feel" emotions such as sadness, joy, or stress in your body and not just in your mind, it's because of a flood of neurochemical activity throughout the body leads to changes in not only how you *think,* but also in the functioning of cells throughout your body. These changes are what Candace Pert describes in her book *Molecules of Emotion*, which refers to the tiny neuropeptides that circulate through the body until they find the right receptor, basically serving as a key that unlocks certain sensations or feelings.

Mind/body health is affiliated with the LOA because many of the practices for creating an optimal emotional or energetic state that supports attracting what you want into your life are based in mind/body practices. Mind/body health is the discipline that proves the beneficial nature of practices such as meditation and other forms of focused awareness in helping us not only to experience favorable emotions, but also to uncover creative insights. Like neuroscience (described below), these strategies actually "train" the brain to function more optimally in areas that create peak experiences for us.

Neuroscience. Neuroscience is the study of the brain and nervous system. It examines all the different aspects of how the brain and nerves interact to guide everything from our thoughts and perceptions to how our body functions, how we learn, how we create memories and meaning, and how we interpret sensory input. It is incredibly important in our discussion of the LOA and how it impacts our life because researchers have found that the brain is actually very plastic—it can literally *rewire* itself to perform different functions and experience life in different ways. Brain research is showing just how powerful the mind is in interpreting reality and in setting the stage for future experiences.

(*Brain research is showing just how powerful the mind is in interpreting reality and in setting the stage for future experiences.*)

For instance, studies have shown that subjects who imagined playing the piano had similar changes in the parts of their brains that coordinate the playing as those who had actually played. And studies by Richard Davidson of the University of Wisconsin at Madison found that "adept" meditators (such as Buddhist monks who had spent their lives cultivating the practice) had formed exceptionally strong connections between thinking and feeling when compared to novice meditators (students). The monks had a greater capacity to influence emotion with conscious thought. Even more important, though, was the fact that the monks experienced considerably stronger brain responses in a key section of the brain associated with positive emotion (and considerably weaker brain responses in the corresponding section associated with negative emotion). This finding demonstrates that, with time and practice, you can actually rewire the structure of the brain, which can effectively "train" the mind to experience more positive states.

This means that we can use conscious choice—and proven practices—to "program" the brain and body to experience and attract more of what we want and less of what we don't want into our lives. Neuroscience is the field that illustrates the power of strategies such as meditation, visualization, and guided imagery (among others) to support the favorable outcomes we seek in life.

We can use conscious choice—and proven practices— to "program" the brain and body to experience and attract more of what we want and less of what we don't want into our lives.

All these fields of study—quantum physics, Positive Psychology, mind/body health, and neuroscience—create a solid infrastructure for us to build a better understanding of *why* the LOA works so that we can then construct a specific action plan for *how* it can work for you. This is where we'll turn our attention to how the science and the strategy behind the LOA can work its magic in our lives. We'll sum it all up in a simple model that describes how it all fits together.

A Different Kind of Super Model

As I started synthesizing the elements of what I appreciate about the popular interpretations of the LOA and combining them with the science and strategy from a variety of disciplines, a model emerged that I thought made the process of mastering the LOA simple and memorable. It's based on the concept that an infinite pool of possibilities and opportunities exist to help you tap into the abundance that life has to offer. In this context, *abundance* refers to everything from peak experiences, favorable emotional states, vibrant physical well-being, fulfilling relationships, financial security, professional success, spiritual centeredness, and a host of other things. Taking a dip in this pool of infinite abundance on a regular basis is what puts the LOA in Action in your life.

When I think of *abundance*, I think of a constant flow of desirable experiences and outcomes in life. And when I think of the *infinite* possibilities and opportunities that exist out there, I always think of the infinity sign from high school math class. Don't worry, folks, this little math lesson will be short, sweet, and purposeful. I promise. The infinity sign is basically a figure eight turned on its side, which is often referred to as a Möbius strip—a symbol that has no beginning and no end. Rather than just being a math symbol, though, it's also a practical way of looking at the way the LOA works.

When I think about the LOA, the infinity sign makes sense to me for two reasons: First, it represents the field of unlimited possibilities in our lives—there is a constant flow of opportunities, where the end of one experience simply represents the beginning of another series of possibilities. Second, the symbol offers a convenient visual reminder about the three key steps in the LOA in Action model:

Step 1. Choose Your State.

Step 2. Set Your Intention.

Step 3. Take Inspired Action.

Your role is to travel continuously through each of these steps with each new intention you set in your life. It's a smooth, flowing journey as you repeatedly travel around that figure eight and experience unprecedented joy, satisfaction, and success in your life. The following diagram illustrates this "Different Kind of Super Model" and a detailed description of each step follows.

Step 1. Choose Your State. I couldn't be more convinced that choosing your state is the critical foundation that makes every other aspect of the LOA work. This basically means that you *consciously* decide how you want to feel emotionally—the energy you want to experience and project out into the world—and then take consistent steps to create as favorable an emotional state as you can in any given moment. The reason choosing your state is so integral to your success in applying the LOA is that unless you are *consciously* choosing to direct your thoughts and energy in constructive ways, you won't be able to identify and envision powerful *intentions* (desires that will transform your life). And you will be equally incapable of taking *inspired action* to realize those outcomes. In fact, if you aren't careful about the state you choose, you will more than likely subconsciously create a "vicious cycle" that attracts to you more of the same negative emotions, situations, and people.

On the contrary, if you consciously choose your state, you will create a "virtuous cycle" in your life that starts with experiencing favorable emotions, which help foster favorable results, which then trigger more favorable emotions . . . you get the picture. For instance, if you want to attract a new client or sale in your business, it serves you well to put yourself into a positive state that

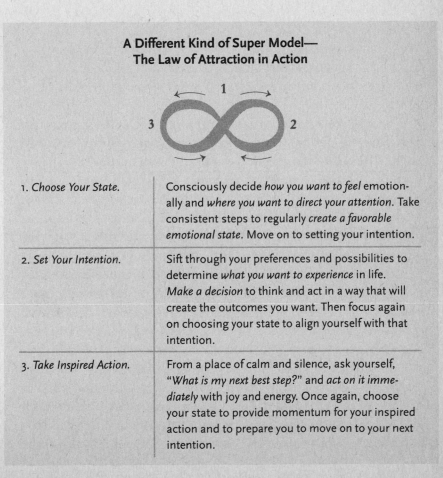

A Different Kind of Super Model— The Law of Attraction in Action

1. *Choose Your State.*	Consciously decide *how you want to feel* emotionally and *where you want to direct your attention.* Take consistent steps to regularly *create a favorable emotional state.* Move on to setting your intention.
2. *Set Your Intention.*	Sift through your preferences and possibilities to determine *what you want to experience* in life. *Make a decision* to think and act in a way that will create the outcomes you want. Then focus again on choosing your state to align yourself with that intention.
3. *Take Inspired Action.*	From a place of calm and silence, ask yourself, "*What is my next best step?*" and *act on it* immediately with joy and energy. Once again, choose your state to provide momentum for your inspired action and to prepare you to move on to your next intention.

helps you feel energized about your product or service. If your state conveys apathy or anxiety, it's a pretty sure bet that your prospective client will seek out one of the many other resources that could meet his needs. We've all had the experience of being so repelled by a salesperson's negative vibe that we made a beeline for the door at the first opportunity. Choosing your state either sets the stage for success or delivers predictable disappointment.

> *Choosing your state is the critical foundation that makes every other aspect of the LOA work.*

Step 2. Set Your Intention. Setting your intention is the strategy that helps you sift through your preferences and possibilities, and then decide with clarity and conviction what you want to experience in life. Intention is about knowing with certainty what you want, and believing that it is possible to have it. It is the magic moment of *decision*— deciding that things will be different and that you will be an instrument to make that happen. Intention is also about making a *choice* to consciously and consistently think and act in ways that will create the results you want in life. How you approach intention is the most accurate predictor of your experience. As an example, your intention for an interaction with another person (spouse, child, friend) often determines the outcome of that interaction. If you go into a situation expecting tension or frustration, disappointment or distress, you will undoubtedly get exactly what you expect. How many times have you feared—no, expected—that things weren't going to go well and, as if by magic, they didn't? That's because you set the *intention* for that to happen, so the situation follows that natural path. If, on the other hand, you enter into the conversation with an intention to be relaxed and open rather than guarded or jaded, you can often create an entirely different—and far more pleasant—result than you otherwise would. As Wayne Dyer says, "Our intention creates our reality," so be thoughtful about the intentions you set!

(*Intention is about knowing with certainty what you want, and believing that it is possible to have it.*)

Step 3. Take Inspired Action. Taking inspired action is often the step in LOA work that many people tend to gloss over for some reason. In fact, many of the existing books and videos on the LOA focus extensively—almost exclusively—on paying attention to *how* you are thinking (choosing your state) and on *what* you are thinking about (setting your intention) to the exclusion of taking inspired action. Indeed, choosing your state and setting your intention are critical elements of the LOA—it just doesn't work if you leave them out—but the fact remains that *thinking* doesn't usually yield practical and tangible results. That's the reason why *New* Year's resolutions perpetually become *Next* Year's resolutions—because people tend to *think* about them more than act on them. It's *action* that produces results. The important distinction, though, is that we're talking here about *inspired* action, as opposed to arduous, exhausting, painstaking action. Inspired action is based on what you intuitively know will be your "next best step." The word choice is important here. It's your next *best* step—the one that energizes and delights you, rather than making you feel like you "must get through" *this* in order to experience or be rewarded with *that*. In the words of LOA practitioner and author Joe Vitale, "Inspired action is any action you take based on an inside nudge."

Inspired action comes from a place of calm and silence in your mind, which fosters the creativity you need to spark insight and inspiration.

> (*Inspired action is based on what you intuitively know will be your "next best step."*)

You can think about this model the way you think about cultivating a garden. When you plant a garden, your *state* includes all the things that set the stage for plants to grow and thrive—good soil, plenty of water and sunshine, and nutrients that support their well-being. No matter how much you want to see a thriving garden, it just won't happen if you neglect to put the basic foundations in place for it to grow. Your *intention*, then, is the type of seeds or starters you select, which represent the specific outcomes you want to achieve in life. In a garden, if you want squash, you plant squash. You don't plant strawberries and expect squash to sprout. (If you do, you willingly set yourself up for a mighty disappointing harvest.) Likewise, you don't throw in a bunch of random seeds and "imagine" your way toward the specific crop you want. For the results you want, you get clear about what you want to produce, choose the right seeds and starters, and then act. In a garden, the *inspired action* includes the habits and behaviors you implement from the day you prepare the soil and sow the seeds to the day your intention comes to fruition. It includes your responses to environmental conditions, your active attention to the well-being of the garden, and the thoughtful tending of your intentions as you steward them toward their destiny. This could be the habit of watering and weeding, of protecting plants from frost or critters, of thinning out the crop to allow the rest of the blooms to thrive, and the like. All these things are necessary if the garden is to thrive, and all these steps are necessary if your life is to thrive as a result of using the LOA in Action.

Where Do We Go from Here?

The rest of the book explores each of the three elements of the LOA in Action model: Choose Your State, Set Your Intention, and Take Inspired Action. In the remainder of Part One, you will be introduced to detailed descriptions of the concepts themselves, giving you a clear understanding of *how* the LOA works. In Part Two, you will learn various strategies that will help you customize and apply each concept in your life, showing you how the LOA can work for you.

Your most significant role as you read this book is to sample the array of information and offerings and then to tailor your approach to learning and applying the LOA based on your unique preferences and interests. This model is not a one-size-fits-all approach to living the LOA. On the contrary, I encourage you to try things on for size and see how they feel. Your first test for each strategy will be whether or not it sparks an immediate interest for you. Try these first—there's a reason you are intuitively drawn to these methods. But I caution you *not* to dismiss the others at first glance. You might want to give all of them a try, because often we don't know what we will like or how these methods might transform our lives until we sample them for ourselves, much like our experience with a new food or skill or hobby. Sometimes it's a matter of exploring something new before it becomes intriguing—and promising—enough to embrace.

Throughout Part Two, you will also find worksheets that help you not only *understand* and *practice* the new strategy, but also *reflect* on its impact on your life. You will hear stories of how others have used these concepts and strategies to make a difference in their lives so that you can see the range of opportunities to use the LOA to your benefit. I hope you will give yourself the gift of time and creative focus to work through the exercises as you go, rather than simply reading the book and then coming back to complete the exercises later. As its title suggests, this book is meant to help you put the LOA into *Action*, not into a perpetual holding pattern in your brain or your life. So I encourage you to *take action as you go* to ensure you fully understand and skillfully apply the concepts. That's where the status quo ends and transformation begins—no matter where you're starting from. If you commit to testing the strategies as you go, it will serve as a "layering" process for your learning, allowing you to master important concepts and practices one at a time and to apply them in your life for the greatest benefit. In my years of practice as a speaker and coach, I have found that this form of "layered learning" is what yields the most powerful—and the most lasting—results. At the end of the book you will also find a list of the very best resources I know for exploring the different elements of the LOA, integrating them into your life, and experiencing the remarkable, lasting results you're after.

> *Action is where the status quo ends and transformation begins—no matter where you're starting from.*

So have at it! Immerse yourself in the material, engage yourself in the learning, and enjoy yourself in the process. Remember, it's as much about being present on the journey as it is about reaching the destination. Here's to a great trip!

CHAPTER TWO

Rejoice in the Choice:
Choosing Your State

Extreme Makeover: Attitude Edition

I'd love to say that I've always operated in some Zen-like state of personal control and psychological empowerment. But I laugh even as I write that, and even more so when I imagine my previous experiences to the contrary, when overcommitted slammed headlong into overwhelmed. Not a pretty pileup. Things are different now, though, thanks to the LOA. That's why I like to share my own experiences as I apply the very best of the LOA principles in my life. I know it works. Today's evidence: *Extreme Makeover: Attitude Edition.*

The "before" picture of my Extreme Makeover emerged over the course of a week, with the help of a loyal group of friends and an odd little conference activity. It came only days after I had stayed up most of the night in an insomniac frenzy of list writing and strategizing about how the bejeebers I was going to follow through on all my commitments. I was starting to think that the only likely outcome would be *less* of a commitment to my *deliver-*

ables and *more* of a commitment to a *medical facility* where people speak softly and encourage you to complete your latch-hook project.

I had mind-mapped everything from my business to my baby girl's needs and had bulleted my talking points, brownie points, and breaking points for just about every life area. I turned to yoga, warm milk, and fragrant lavender baths, but every attempt to seduce the elusive sleep genie left me stretched, satiated, and sweet-smelling, but even more alert than before. I was a frenetic list-making machine.

The next day happened to be one of my twice-monthly calls to my mastermind team—a mighty group of great thinkers dedicated to helping me stay successful . . . and at times . . . sane. On this particular day, I wept bitter tears as I recounted how I had wept bitter tears the night before, filled with anxiety about what *needed to be done* and how I felt so completely *undone*. My mission was to help others but I seemed incapable of helping myself gain clarity and control.

My group listened patiently and then, with a gentle flourish, served me a hearty helping of insight. Their touching blend of compassion and raw objectivity (how did they do that?) suggested that this overwhelm, this frenzy of mine, was somewhat of a . . . *pattern* for me (insert dramatic music and camera close-up here). They noticed that things would be humming along brilliantly in my life and business and then, *wham*, all hell would break loose and I'd collapse in a sniveling freak-out-a-thon. Usually, they said, I would crescendo to a brief but most unpleasant level of chaos, quickly and efficiently implode, and then pick myself up, do a little strategizing, and get back on the path again until the next episode.

They all asked some version of the question "So, when are you going to decide *not to go there anymore?*" In this case "there" meant descending into the emotional abyss, where I adopted the characteristics of a rather lovable but tortured alter ego overwhelmed by everything and everyone. This, I think, is the part of the reality program where the subject realizes that "something simply *must* change!" and that *now* is the time for said change to occur. Only, on extreme makeover programs, a huge semitruck pulls up with great fanfare and out jump hundreds of eager volunteers poised to renovate their house. Or a motor home emerges from the fog, carting a parade of "experts" to cure what ails them—doctors, chefs, trainers, coaches, pet-psychics, and ghost-whisperers.

If only it were that easy . . . or prime-time friendly. For me, the revelation did *not* come complete with stream of specialists to "fix" me or my situation and leave me with a year's supply of laundry detergent or the nubile body of a perky coed many years my junior. I realized in that moment that I had to *design my own Extreme Makeover*, comprised of an imaginary little team of experts to swoop in and stitch up my psyche. The nice thing, though, was that I could choose to forgo Dr. Phil in favor of Dr Pepper, and if I wanted to, my interior designer could outfit my outlook and my landscape artist could prune my perspective. "Hmmmm," I thought, "there might be something to this Extreme Makeover."

It was tough to admit but true—it was time for a radical change in my outlook and my life, and only *I* could orchestrate it. I thought about it and decided that *now* would be the time I would decide "*not to go there anymore,*" and that I would use my mastermind group's help and our upcoming trip to a great seminar to commit to "choosing my state" from here on out. Basically, that meant that *I* wanted to be the one controlling my thoughts, my decisions, and my actions to draw more of what I wanted into my life, rather than allowing myself to be a victim, recklessly tossed around by external pressures or unproductive thinking.

The Transformation Begins

At the seminar, one of my tasks was to make a list of the ways I tended to limit myself—the things I do, or the ways I think, that create barriers to my success. I made what, at that time, had become a fairly common list for me—what I dubbed the "Tyranny of Too's and To-Do's." The list went a little something like this: "I take on *too* much at once. I say yes *too* often when I want to say no. I pack *too* much into my schedule. I commit to *too* many *to-do's*. I get *too* overwhelmed and frenzied," and so on. But it was the next part that really grabbed me. Once I made that list of "limiting thoughts and behaviors," I was charged with creating a stage or movie character that represented all these things. This character needed to walk, talk, act, and think *exactly* in the ways I tended to limit myself. I was told to name this person and get a very clear picture of how she would act.

I knew immediately what I would call my alter ego: "Ms. Big-Ass Frenzy of the Month" (with "Big-Ass" referring, of course, to the *frenzy*, not to the *Ms.*). I envisioned her caught up in a whirlwind of unfinished projects and emails, with ringing cell phones and file folders swooping around her like vultures. She looked like a moderately hygienic, tech-savvy Pig Pen from the *Peanuts* cartoons, with a cloud of chaos following her everywhere. She'd be flitting about in this portable tumult to the tune of "Flight of the Bumblebee," blaring, of course, from an iPod that also haphazardly circled her.

She would talk like a Valley Girl, high on three quad lattes with a Red Bull chaser, saying things like "Oh my GOSH. I can't, like, BELIEVE how much I have to DO. I am SO overWHELMED and filled with total, like, ANGST. I am FREAKING OUT. I totally, can't, like, SLEEP. Oh my GOSH. I'm supposed to be totally

HELPING people but even though I've mind-mapped my whole, like, LIFE and counted sheep and my blessings and my to-do list like fifty TIMES, I still can't SLEEP. Maybe if I count BACKWARD and FORWARD at the same time, it will totally, like, SHORT-CIRCUIT my BRAIN. 100, 1, 99, 2, 98, 3 . . . OHMYGOSH . . . I just thought of three more things I have to, like, DO . . ." and so on. You get the picture.

I giggled to myself in the middle of that huge auditorium because this was *exactly* what I felt like in one of those "Ms. Big-Ass Frenzy" moments, down to the counting forward and backward strategy, which I literally had tried only a few nights before. In case you're wondering . . . it didn't work. The absurdity of my "alter ego" was so vivid that I actually got up on stage and portrayed her for hundreds of people in an effort to solidify just how ridiculous it would be to knowingly *choose* to live even one more moment in this state. I finally had realized that how I felt about myself and my life was entirely up to me. *It was my choice.* We were then told that, in our role as director of our lives, we could simply cut this character from the cast and replace her with one who behaves in ways that support—rather than undermine—our success and fulfillment. Time for a casting call!

I made the decision then and there to bid a long overdue farewell to this character, rather than recruiting a legion of experts to try to "fix" her. I decided I'd write into my life makeover a character who made great, empowered decisions about *how to choose her emotional and physical state* to attract better outcomes in her life. She would consciously decide which perspective she wanted to choose, which emotional "set point" she wanted to select, and which physical energy state she wanted to create at any given time. I would no longer allow Ms. Big-Ass Frenzy to make unbidden repeat appearances in my life as my evil twin or my archenemy.

The Reveal

I orchestrated my own Extreme Makeover—Attitude Edition. I put a few things in place that I knew would support me in choosing my state and attracting what I want—rather than what I don't want—into my life. I've found that a few simple practices for choosing my state have made a world of difference in my life experience, and I've found that it gets easier to use them all the time. "Ms. Big-Ass Frenzy of the Month" was written out of the script months ago. I replaced her with "Ms. Bask in My Bliss Right Now." I find that Ms. Now has a growing fan club and record-shattering ratings, and has won critical acclaim for attracting not overwhelm *itself*, but rather an almost overwhelming degree of *life satisfaction and success*. And she didn't even need a team of well-meaning experts to fix her up. She just needed to choose her state . . . every day . . . to set the stage for living life on her own terms. And you can do the same. Let's take a look at how.

State—The Facts

What is *state* anyway, and why the heck would you want to choose it? Dictionary definitions, with their uncanny knack for making things exceptionally lackluster, describe *state* as "a mode or condition of being" and "a condition of mind or temperament." This translates into the idea of simply naming *how you are feeling at any given time*, emotionally, physically, and even spiritually. I prefer to think of state, though, as *the all-powerful combination of thoughts, beliefs, and emotions that make absolutely everything possible.*

(State *is the all-powerful combination of thoughts, beliefs, and emotions that make absolutely everything possible.*)

Are you feeling optimistic, energetic, and engaged? Filled with eager anticipation for all the new opportunities life has to offer you? Hopped up on joy and possibility? Or are you feeling pessimistic, lethargic, and apathetic? Angst-ridden and ready to crawl under a rock somewhere? Overwhelmed at the sheer injustice of what life keeps throwing your way? All these words and phrases describe *states*, it's just that some tend to make you swoon with unbridled delight, and others, with nausea at the very thought of feeling them for even a minute longer. Time for the test. Which of these states would make you leap to your feet and scream, "Hook me up with another dose of that, please!" Well, that list is the one that can transform your life. It's all about making a conscious decision to choose your state.

It's time for an important disclaimer here. It's not to say that "positive" emotions are "good" and that "negative" emotions are "bad," it's really more about *how you use* your emotions. Uncomfortable states or emotions serve a purpose—to provide contrast and clarity about what doesn't feel quite right in your life. They are meant to be tools for exploration and learning, for enlightenment and redirection. They are meant to be alarm clocks or stop signs or searchlights or invitations that draw your attention to something that can benefit from change.

When you feel stressed or overwhelmed, it could be a signal that either your schedule and commitments are out of whack or your priorities are out of balance (or both). When you feel anger or resentment, it could be a sign that you are not attending to your own needs or you have a clash of values or respect with someone or something else. When you feel helpless or hopeless, it could be telling you that you aren't taking ownership of your opportunities to influence a situation, or that you might want to call in reinforcements to support you through a challenging situation. Every emotion or state is different, every person is different, and every way of interpreting what you can learn is different. That's what makes the world go around.

But the most important goal is *not to allow yourself to get mired up in and paralyzed by negative emotions*. It's a fact that bad things absolutely do happen to good people, and that pain and grief and disappointment and anger are all parts of being human. Welcome to the unpredictable adventure called life! The point is that these experiences or emotions *do not have to define who you are or what your life is destined to feel like forever*. The fact is, we only know happiness in contrast to its opposite—sadness—and we only identify stress because, conversely, we can readily recognize balance. Big contrast provides big clarity about what you *do* want to feel or experience. The key is to thoughtfully choose the meaning you attribute to everything that happens in your life, and then to make a choice about where you want to go from here.

> *Big contrast provides big clarity about what you* do *want to feel or experience.*

The field of Positive Psychology tells us that it is your *choice* to allow your responses to events and emotions to either *anchor you where you are now* (experiencing what you *don't* want to experience and stuck where you *don't* want to be) or to *springboard you toward where you want to be* (experiencing what you *do* want to experience and moving toward where you *do* want to be). One choice keeps you in your dead-end job living paycheck to paycheck, while another leads to a fulfilling career and a fabulous lifestyle. One choice keeps you smothered in an unfulfilling relationship, while another stokes the fires of satisfaction. One choice keeps you stressed and stretched and sanity-starved, while another leads to your unique blend of balance and bliss. In each case, one of these options sounds far more appealing than the other, don't you think? So as you choose your state, you simply want to look for opportunities to think rationally and productively, creatively and proactively, despite your circumstances. As you do this, you will consistently build strength that will help you skillfully navigate misfortune and draw positive experiences of all kinds into your life.

While choosing your state implies that you make a *conscious* decision about how you want to feel at any given time, choosing a state that *serves* you is a far more important part of the equation. It's kind of like selecting your favorite television show rather than channel surfing. When you channel surf, you're *consciously choosing to mindlessly scan* what's out there, not really invested in—or necessarily interested in—what flashes across the screen. But when you tune into your favorite show, you are *consciously choosing to purposefully watch*, fully present to the experience. One act is passive, the other is active. And as you'll continue to see, it's *active* participation in life that yields more of what you want.

(*It's active participation in life that yields more of what you want.*)

You are actually controlling your state all the time, most often unconsciously, by allowing your moods and feelings to be dictated by (or at least unduly influenced by) outside circumstances, other people, and at times even your own inner dialogue. Whether it's an untimely traffic jam, a moody spouse, or the pity party of the century, many people hop aboard the *S.S. Mindless* for frequent tours around the harbor of discontent. Alternatively, when you practice the art of *deliberately* choosing your state—consciously *deciding* where you want to focus your attention and *selecting* the type of energy you want to bathe yourself in—you can find yourself cruising off to explore exotic lands on the luxury liner *Contentment*. Now that puts you in a much more powerful position to attract—and enjoy—the things you want into your life.

Choosing your state is the single most important element of putting the LOA in Action, because it sets the stage for effectively stating your intentions and efficiently taking inspired action to achieve them. By choosing your state, you "prime the pump" to draw a rich array of favorable life experiences and (equally as important) to enjoy the process of manifesting them. Just as priming the pump allows you to enjoy both that drink of water *and* a feeling of refreshment, remember that a vibrant, satisfying life is as much about your experience in *living* as it is about what you *achieve*.

Perhaps the most important point is to make it a practice to always acknowledge that *you have a choice*—the option of choosing your state, regardless of your outside circumstances. Remember that by exercising that choice, you maximize the forces of energy within yourself (and in your interactions with others and the Universe) to conspire on your behalf to create the life experiences and outcomes you desire. It's the ultimate in self-fulfilling prophecies.

On Choosing Your State

Often, when people talk about the LOA, they refer to choosing your state as "raising your vibration," referencing the quantum physics principle that "everything is energy." So they say that when you "raise your vibration," you supposedly elevate your energy to a higher level, which "magnetizes" you to attract more of what you want. Or they refer to the idea that your task is to select the right frequency on your vibrational tuner to receive the signal of the Universe on a radio station that plays an assortment of continuous hits—your dreams and aspirations. According to some proponents, when we do this, what we want is magically attracted to us by some unseen force. This description ranks a little high on the "woo-woo" meter to me. I tend toward thinking more along the lines of what some LOA practitioners refer to as "resonance" and "harmony."

Resonance is the notion of producing a particular vibration in a system. When two guitars are tuned the same, if you pluck a string on one guitar, the corresponding string on the nearby guitar will begin to vibrate, too. So, in your practice of choosing your state, one of your goals would be to create *resonance* in your life with the things you want to *experience more of.* This is the reason you choose to "vibrate" in resonance with experiencing optimism or gratitude and to release from your mind the vibrations of lack or pessimism—so that when you pluck an emotional string, it will resonate with corresponding experiences that you want to draw into your life, rather than with those you don't. It's a good practice to focus on resonating with thoughts and images of vibrant well-being rather than illness, with successful and satisfying business ventures rather than fear of failure, and with joyful parenting rather than overwhelm and struggle.

Harmony means "a pleasing or congruent arrangement of parts, or accord." Harmony occurs when you play musical notes around a melody, which can radically change the sound of the melody itself and the "feel" of the entire piece of music. Choosing your state involves purposefully selecting the harmony you attach to whatever melody is playing in your life. If the melody is a pleasing one, you can enhance it and enrich it with the notes (the thoughts and perceptions) that you add to it. If it's an unpleasant one, you can transform it simply by thoughtfully selecting the notes (again, your thoughts and perceptions) that you want to surround it. Thus, you can create harmony in your life by connecting with others to celebrate great moments (thereby *enhancing* your experience), or to gain needed support during challenging times (thereby *transforming* your experience). Harmony is always possible when you are thoughtful about selecting the right notes for yourself and the outcomes you desire.

These concepts are more about *aligning* and *enhancing* your emotional state with what it is that you want to experience *more* of in your life, as opposed to achieving a "high vibration," which could be contradictory at times to what you might want to experience. For instance, you may want to experience peace and tranquility, silence and relaxation, all of which are pleasant and sought-after vibrations, but aren't necessarily associated with the notion of a *high* vibration. Choosing your state is more about selecting a vibration that is *congruent* with what you want.

Choosing your state is also a matter of aligning yourself with the emotional and physical resources you need to identify and act on your preferences and desires. A favorable state makes you more creative, more inspired, and more likely to be clear about what you want. It also helps you take action and cultivate habits and practices that support realizing your dreams.

A favorable state makes you more creative, more inspired, and more likely to be clear about what you want. It also helps you take action and cultivate habits and practices that support realizing your dreams.

There are so many favorable emotional states to choose from, and it really boils down to consistently *choosing a state conducive to attracting your desired outcomes.* This could mean choosing states of gratitude and appreciation, optimism and hope, energy and eagerness, love and compassion, or peace and balance (among others). All support different types of results in your life, and all are desirable at different times and in different ways. It's pretty obvious that if you want to draw quality experiences, people, and things into your life, it's far more likely to happen when you are in one of these favorable emotional and energetic states.

Choosing a favorable state helps you achieve outcomes in your life the same way that deciding how you'll use your car will support the outcomes you want to achieve in a day. Some days, you'll be taking a leisurely drive through the park to soak up the scenery and bask in the pleasure of the moment. You don't need to rev your engine to experience what you want to. Some days you'll use it for practical errands that make your life easier, so you'll want the capacity to start and stop repeatedly to make smooth transitions between each destination. Some days you'll hit the freeway and shift into overdrive to take the fast track toward a great destination. And some days, if someone you care about is ill or injured, you want to be able to use your car to get to the emergency room quickly and safely to get care for them. There are so many ways that you could use your car—you only need to know what state serves the outcome you're seeking in each instance. The same holds true for your emotional state—you just need to know how to choose your state and how to easily navigate in and out of states that serve the purposes most important to you at a given time.

Energizing the Attraction Machine

A few key concepts help make the whole attraction machine work: (1) Everything is energy; (2) thoughts are the most powerful form of energy; and (3) when you change your state, you change both your *current experience* and your *future outcomes*.

1. *Everything is energy.* As I've already discussed at length, quantum physics tells us that everything is energy. Whether you're talking about a tree, a table, your thumb, or a thought, at its most basic level it's just a mass of energy vibrating at a specific frequency. Once you realize that everything is energy, you can decide how you want to use your physical and psychological resources to *consciously* design your life experience.

> *Once you realize that everything is energy, you can decide how you want to use your physical and psychological resources to* consciously *design your life experience.*

2. *Thoughts are the most powerful form of energy—and you can change them.* Just like the energy pulsing through the wires of your home can be channeled, interrupted, and redirected through switches and sockets, cords and machines, so can your energy. The only difference is that your energy is channeled, interrupted, and redirected through your attention and thoughts, your choices and your actions. It is through this redirection of energy that you influence your state. Thoughts are the most

powerful forms of energy, and you can change them—and your outcomes—in a fraction of a second. Neuroscience research proves that when you think certain thoughts, they activate certain muscles in the body. Mind/body studies have shown that distinct ways of thinking immediately impact stress hormones in the body, the functioning of the immune system, and even your heart rhythms. Positive Psychology has shown that optimism and gratitude practices readily impact the immune system and depression rates. As soon as you think a thought, you begin to change your state and to influence your experience, whether positively or negatively, desired or undesired, conscious or unconscious. But it doesn't stop with your experience right now.

Thoughts are the most powerful forms of energy, and you can change them—and your outcomes—in a fraction of a second.

3. *When you change your state, you change both your current experience and your future outcomes.* The quality of your thoughts and the images you hold in your mind influence both your present moment and your future results in life. For instance, neuroscience studies have shown that visualization changes how the body's muscles respond *right now*, and also impacts the individual's performance *in the future*. Likewise, mind/body experts have proven that strategies such as meditation not only change the stress response in the body *in the present moment* but also contribute not just to *slowing* but actually to *reversing* heart disease *in the future* for patients following a particular medical program. And the Positive Psychology research mentioned above has shown that regular gratitude practices enhance happiness both *today* and *over time*, and that learning to be optimistic

decreases depression, improves health outcomes, and enhances workplace success on many levels *now* and for many *years to come*. With evidence like this, it makes infinite sense to learn how to choose your state. Let's take a look at how that's done.

(*The quality of your thoughts and the images you hold in your mind influence both your present moment and your future results in life.*)

Traveling on the "Inner State"

So by now you know that you can readily learn to choose your state by consciously *directing your thoughts and making a decision*. You can master proven strategies that put you into a "peak state" that corresponds with your desired outcomes, whether those outcomes involve health, wealth, love, happiness, or success. In effect, your state helps create your own personal gravitational pull to attract more of what you want—and less of what you don't want—into your life.

Always remember that the *only* things you have control over in any circumstance are your own thoughts, including the meaning you ascribe to what you observe, and the action you decide to take to influence your situation.

(*The only things you have control over in any circumstance are your own thoughts.*)

That's it. The good thing is that the more skilled you become at *recognizing* and *responding* to these facts, the more likely you are to regularly be in an emotional state that draws more desirable experiences, people, and things into your life.

There are two great categories of activities that can help support your efforts to consciously choose your state: GIGO and Spacemakers. While the specific strategies will be described in detail in Part Two, the following is a brief overview of what they are.

GIGO

You've probably heard of the notion of GIGO, which means "garbage in, garbage out." For our purposes, we'll take it to mean "good in, good out." It's really a matter of being thoughtful about what you put *into* your mind and body because that determines what flows *out* of your mind and into your life experience. Just as what you put into your body impacts your physical well-being, your choice of mental nutrition will either strengthen or taint your state, and thus your outcomes. When I refer to "good in, good out," I'm not suggesting that you adopt "Don't Worry, Be Happy" as your personal theme song. That would likely set you up for extreme social isolation. What "good in" really means is that you are *selective* about what you allow to enter into your conscious thought.

(*It's really a matter of being thoughtful about what you put into your mind and body because that will determine what flows out of your mind and into your life experience.*)

If there were a magic pill for living a more joyful, productive, healthy life, the active ingredient would be "good in." Pharmaceutical companies would be falling all over themselves to create sexy ads to entice the public to storm medical offices demanding their fix. Likewise, medical practitioners would be gladly writing lifetime prescriptions for a happy pill that had no risk of spurring malpractice suits. Alas, the magic *pill doesn't* exist (much to the pharmaceutical companies' dismay, no doubt), but the magic *practice does*, in the form of choosing your state and specifically allowing "good in, good out." It's one of the most powerful ways to change your state and to truly experience joy in the moment.

What's even more compelling, though, is that choosing your state isn't just about feeling good *emotionally*. What you decide to put into your mind has an immediate and profound effect on your body, on molecules outside the body, and subsequently on all sorts of outcomes. For instance, research has found that there is a clear and consistent system of communication between the mind and the body. In one set of studies focusing on the link between thoughts and the heart, researchers found that negative emotions literally set off a chain reaction of damaging effects in the body, including the release of stress hormones, increases in blood pressure, the creation of irregular heart rhythms, a weakening of the immune system, and a host of other unfavorable outcomes. In return, the heart sends even more information to the brain than the brain sends to the heart, which then proceeds to drain our energy and focus, perpetuating even more negative emotions. This starts the whole cycle all over again.

Another array of fascinating experiments conducted by Dr. Masuro Emoto is described in books such as *The Hidden Messages in Water* and *The Secret Life of Water*. In these experiments, Emoto examined the structure of water molecules after they were exposed to a variety of different energies, emotions, words, music, and other influences (he uses the term *hado*, which translates to "vibration"). What Emoto found was that when water was exposed to positive energies and emotions (including words like "love and gratitude," "thank you," and "wisdom"), the water crystals formed from the frozen sample exhibited beautiful, complete, artful, snowflake-like patterns. When the samples were exposed to words like "you make me sick," "you fool," and even to commands such as "do it" (as opposed to the more cooperative "let's do it"), the crystals appeared distorted, incomplete, and even disturbing. The implications of these findings are striking . . . if words, energies, and emotions can impact water crystals in this way, what might be the impact on our bodies, minds, and the planet as a whole, all of which consist of at least 70 percent water?

These research findings suggest that we have a great deal of power at our disposal to influence our energy and state (and therefore our life experience) by being selective about what we put into our minds. GIGO strategies (described in Part Two) make it simple and methodical to consciously choose what you allow to enter your mind, how those things influence your state, and how your state impacts your results in life.

(*We have a great deal of power at our disposal to influence our energy and state (and therefore our life experience) by being selective about what we put into our minds.*)

Spacemakers

While GIGO strategies focus on what you put *into* your mind, Spacemaker strategies focus on what you *release*. Spacemakers are in a way related to how you approach your filing system. A filing

cabinet can only hold so much and still allow you to use it efficiently. Sure, you can keep jamming papers in there until you need
the Jaws of Life to retrieve anything. Right about this time, though,
all your key documents can start getting damaged, distorted, or
lost in the chaos. Not only that, but you certainly don't have room
to bring in anything new and exciting to make your life easier or
more interesting, so you revert to using dated information (or just
making stuff up as you go along) or you spend inordinate amounts
of time trying to find something important in the mess. As an alternative, you allow the piles and piles of paper to engulf your desk,
your office, and your life without producing any meaningful outcomes. None of these options seems overly productive.

The reality is that your mind is a lot like your filing system. You
need to *make space* for what you really *want* to keep in there. If
you keep it stuffed full of thoughts and beliefs that don't serve you
anymore, or packed with dated information and perceptions that
worked for you when you were eight but don't come close to helping you out now, your mind will go the way of the overstuffed filing cabinet. You won't be able to find what you need when you
need it, or you won't even go looking for it. And you certainly
won't be able to replace missing or lost information because there's
no room for it anyway. The fact is that if you want to be enriching
your marriage or healing your body or making your millions, it can
be kind of hard to do those things while buried alive under a heap-
ing pile of everything you don't need anymore.

There's only so much room in our minds to hold emotions and
awareness that we can readily get to and actually use. That's
because the brain's reticular activating system (RAS) serves as a
little filing system that stores all the "important" and "frequently
used" files at the front of the drawer. Anything you regularly focus
your attention on, whether it's constructive or not and whether

you're conscious of it or not, goes into these files for ready access. This goes for emotions, beliefs, perceptions, assessments, whatever.

Those "important" files often contain old emotional traumas that we've never fully processed, or habitual ways of thinking that undermine our efforts to change our lives. They can contain beliefs that we formed about the world, other people, or ourselves that actually have no foundation in fact because we learned them unconsciously when we were very young. They can contain mistaken perceptions of what we have to do, who we have to be, and how we measure up. And think about it . . . if those files contain primarily these types of *negative* patterns of thinking, how or where or when will you be able to make room for new, more *productive* ways of thinking? You've got to create *space* to accommodate new ways of *thinking* and new ways of *being*. The best way to do this is to purge your files of what you don't need anymore to make room for what you do. You do this by practicing powerful techniques to release what's not working for you so that you can *embrace what can work for you* if you give it a chance.

> *You've got to create space to accommodate new ways of thinking and new ways of being.*

Spacemaker strategies integrate proven techniques that address how the mind and body process challenges, store "memories" (hint . . . your cells remember just as much as your mind does!), and work together either to shut down in the face of difficulty or to create a pathway for evolving into new opportunities. By using Spacemakers periodically, you create the room and order in your mind to choose your state more readily and more completely. In Part Two, you will learn a host of GIGO and Spacemaker strategies that can readily change both your *state* and your *life*. In the meantime, we'll look at a few stories of others who have experienced the power of choosing their state.

Examples Abound: The Power of Choosing Your State

There are a myriad of examples of how choosing—or not choosing—your state can impact your ability to attract what you want into your life. The following are a few tales that give you a sense of the diversity of approaches for choosing state and the outcomes that can be associated with doing it effectively or, in one case, doing it ineffectively.

What a Trip. Jessica, a savvy, charming waitress I know, was experiencing major financial constraints just before her very first trip away from her family. Although she'd made a huge stride in actually deciding to indulge in a little self-care for the first time in her life, she had been struggling under the pressure of the economic burden that it seemed the trip would be. She would have to miss shifts, and as a waitress she didn't get paid if she didn't work. Jessica would have the expense of the trip itself which, although pretty modest, was a cost she wasn't used to budgeting. She would be diverting funds from what could be used for various things the kids wanted or needed. She was convinced she wanted to go, and that it was timely in her life. But she felt tremendous anxiety about how it would all come together and how on earth she would afford it.

She decided to focus on changing her state about the trip by releasing her anxiety and focusing on the tremendous gratitude she had for what was already present in her life. She chose a state of peace, calm, and certainty that everything would work out as it should and directed her energy toward being upbeat and energized about the trip instead of anxious and overwhelmed. The very day she shifted her focus, out of the blue, Terry, one of her regular customers, left her a $500 tip with a sweet note. The note simply encouraged her to enjoy herself on the trip that would no doubt change her life. Terry affirmed that Jessica deserved to do something for herself and suggested that one day, when she was in a position to help someone else do the same, to then "pay the favor forward" to help another person out in some way. Jessica drew unexpected support and collaboration into her life simply by choosing her state.

Physician, Heal Thyself. Jeremy, a gifted physician, was ready to leave the medical profession altogether because he absolutely despised his job and dreaded going to work every day. He regularly fought with his partners, all of whom he felt were "selfish money-hounds." He routinely had heated conflicts with staff and administrators at the hospital where he worked because there were too few resources, too little teamwork, and far too many demands on his time and expertise. He opted to focus on changing his state before deciding to change his profession.

He began a daily practice of gratitude, decided to learn how to integrate more optimism into his interactions with others, and started meditating on a regular basis. He focused his attention on what was good now (or at least improving) in his work, and he became more relaxed in his interactions with his partners and the hospital staff and administrators.

He experienced an almost immediate change in every aspect of his work. Years of "butting heads" were replaced by everyone willingly coming to the table to find solutions to the obvious workload issues. His partners began offering suggestions about how to maintain patient care quality at the same time as quality of life for the physicians, even if that meant spending more money (and thus making less profit) to make it happen—a radical shift in thinking, to be sure. And he found himself recalling what made him go into medicine in the first place, causing him to replace his dread about going to work each day with the appreciation for another "health mystery solved" or another patient and family cared for and comforted. Everything changed when he changed his perspective.

Transitioning Out of Trapped. Melissa was understandably struggling emotionally and financially after her husband had an affair and left their marriage. He left her as a single mom of two young children, working in a job she hated but which she felt she had to keep in order to provide for her kids. She was miserable, bordering on hopeless. She felt trapped in her job, in her caretaker role, and in her negativity. And she felt devastated that her dream of being married and raising her kids with someone she loved was over for now and, she feared, possibly forever.

She made a choice to focus on choosing her state. She decided that she wanted to move her attention *away* from her suffering and pain and *toward* simply being present in her life and conscious of what it had to offer in that very moment, including the opportunity to learn more about herself and how she wanted to live. She wanted to clearly and passionately focus on the fact that she was worthy of being loved—by herself and by a life partner whenever the right person arrived. One year later, she had made a major career transition, felt a profound sense of peace and joy in the moment and in herself, and found herself happily engaged to be married, enjoying a mutually respectful, joyful, loving relationship.

State and Weight. Sharon, Joan, and Debbie wished to reach their ideal weight and experience vibrant well-being. They had struggled with their health and their weight in different ways for many years, and all had "tried just about everything," to no avail. They all began practicing choosing a positive, productive state, including focusing on progress toward their goals rather than stumbling blocks and struggles. Subsequently, all began losing weight with ease while at the same time enhancing their energy and turbocharging their results.

Sharon focused extensively on gratitude, with a mantra of "I am grateful that I am now at my ideal weight," envisioning exactly how it would feel to be at that weight. Joan chose to direct her attention toward practicing the Buddhist principle of "nonviolence" to herself, in the form of eliminating the negative self-talk and judgments she'd struggled with for years. Debbie focused positive energy each day on appreciating aspects of her body as it is right now and focusing with eager anticipation on the changes that were under way.

All were thrilled at the ease with which they approached their weight, but were even more thrilled with their shift in focus and how they *felt* during the *process* of losing the weight. They were happier, healthier, and more successful simply because they reframed how they had always looked at their bodies and their efforts to reach their ideal weight.

Choosing the Wrong State Is Still a Choice. After successfully building his business using Law of Attraction practices, Dan, a business consultant, allowed himself to spiral into a "poor me" slump because he was tired of working an hourly schedule based on other people's demands. After a particularly difficult morning spent thinking about how "I don't want to be sitting there hour after hour based on someone else's schedule and desires," he was in a car crash on the way to the office, sending him straight to the emergency room. The accident resulted in the cancellation of some of his most lucrative clients for the day and sent him into months of medical appointments to treat his injuries. Fortunately, he had a full physical recovery. What he is most grateful for, though, is the recovery of his *attitude* about his business and the *choice* he has about his state.

The accident immediately showed him that he had actually attracted the exact outcome he'd sought that morning. He didn't want to be sitting in front of those clients. By choosing to focus on what he *didn't* want, rather than what he *did* want, he effectively drew a less-than-pleasant outcome that did, indeed, get him out of that office that day. As a result, he began to realize that he could choose to be grateful for the success of his business and what it offered him right now, while still directing positive energy and attention toward shaping it into the type of schedule and work that he wanted to be doing in the future. In the moments after the crash he realized how counterproductive his complaining and pessimism were because, not only did they detract from the enjoyment of his success thus far, but they sucked energy away from his ability to determine what he *did* want and how he could choose his state to be more likely to *receive* it. He began using releasing techniques to let go of negative thinking patterns and replaced them with creative insights that led to outstanding new business ventures.

All these examples point to the fact that the simple act of *choosing your state* sets the stage for *consciously designing the life you want to live*. They are not the end of the story, though . . . they're just the beginning. Because by choosing your state, you readily place yourself in the right mind-set and energetic vibration to set your intention and then take inspired action. We'll move next into exploring the concept of *intention*.

CHAPTER THREE

Preferences, Possibilities, and Certainties: Setting Your Intention

Universal (and Spinal) Alignment

I had been in excruciating back pain for the better part of a week, brought on by the two things that tend to cause spine snafus for me—too much time at the computer and too much time on the road. Okay, because I dwell in honesty, I'll come clean that I hadn't been faithful to my yoga routine for a couple of months, and since it's my elixir for vertebrae vitality and psyche soothing, I was paying for my neglect in more ways than I care to admit.

On the day in question, there I sat in overwhelming discomfort, grimacing every two minutes while I would rather have been fully immersed in the discovery process at a great continuing education event. After a morning of striking various *Vogue*-like poses in the back of the room to relieve the pain radiating down my spine and left arm, the attendees in the back row seemed mildly entertained by my antics—and I was mighty miserable.

For the next exercise, we were supposed to find a partner and ask each other repeatedly, "What are you grateful for?" then record every answer our partner gave. I sat down with a fellow attendee and tried to position myself at an angle that didn't cause convulsions with every breath. I assumed our task would be a pleasant distraction from my pain, so I threw myself into it.

Just a couple of moments into the exercise, I found myself responding to the question with the following statement: "I am grateful that I am in excruciating pain." My partner tilted her head at me like a confused pooch trying to decipher Latin. I was as surprised as she was—these words came out of nowhere and made absolutely no sense.

When I asked myself why this thought had come to mind, I followed it up with, "Because my back is telling me that I haven't been doing *my* part to help bring it into alignment so that it can heal itself." It all boiled down to the fact that I had not been attending to my own wellness and was obviously suffering the consequences. My partner and I nodded in agreement and went on with the exercise. I felt like my subconscious had given me the little epiphany my back had been trying to give me for a week or so, and that my back was seething at me like a brooding teenager, shouting, "You never listen to me!" I made a mental note that I intended to get my back healthy, pain-free, and out of its adolescent moodiness.

At the conclusion of the exercise, a fellow participant at the event asked to purchase a copy of one of my books. Here's a brief response to the questions I know you'll have after I tell this story: I didn't previously know this woman and she hadn't overheard my "back pain revelation."

I sat down on the floor of the auditorium with her to sign the book and we chitchatted for a while. I asked her what she did for a living and she said (this is no lie), "I am a craniosacral therapist. I help people bring their spine and their energy into alignment so that the body can heal itself." I looked up in disbelief, because

twenty minutes earlier I had uttered those very words (or something eerily similar) to a fellow participant, and here I sat with an
individual whose sole purpose in life was to help people like me get
back into a state of health, vitality, and pain-free balance. I looked
for the hidden cameras but didn't find any.

Without telling her my situation, I asked a few more questions
about the science and practice of craniosacral, and wanted to
know a bit more about how it worked. She eloquently described
the practice and her unique approach to it. Then, she started giving
some examples, saying, "For instance, I would put my hand right
here . . ." and as she said that, she placed her hand on the exact
place on my spine that was radiating all the pain. She turned to
look at me and simply said, "Wow, it seems like there's something
going on here." All I could say was, "Uh . . . *yeah*," which was the
understatement of a lifetime. She offered to provide a few minutes
of gentle treatment on my back, there in the middle of a bustling
auditorium, and by the time we were finished, my pain had dimin-
ished by 90 percent.

At this juncture, you might be nodding your head and saying,
"*Riiiigggghhhhtttt*, Deanna. I'm *suuuurrrreeee* that's what happened. Uh-huh. And did Santa Claus come rushing in with a 'Back
in Action' kit and an elfin chiropractor in tow?" But I kid you not
that this exchange really *did* happen, much to my amazement.
While some people might chalk up this experience to coincidence,
serendipity, synchronicity, or dumb luck, I believe that it was a perfect example of the LOA in Action.

I truly believe that because I had started by *choosing a productive state* (being grateful for the messages my body was sending to
me rather than feeling like a victim because I was in so much pain)
and then set my *intention* (to bring my body back into alignment to
allow my spine to heal itself), that's why I readily—and quickly—

attracted this healing resource into my life. If I can draw results like these into my life, I'm convinced that anyone else can, too. It's all about *setting your intention* for what you desire, and that's exactly what this chapter is all about.

A Blueprint for Intention

At its most basic level, intention creates the blueprint from which you can build your future. Just as a blueprint for a new home lays out the picture of how it will turn out, including the aesthetics, the foundation, the structure, and all those little details that polish up the finished product. The wonderful thing about blueprints is that they give you a starting point to work from, but they can be altered. You can add, subtract, or revise elements. You can focus more resources in certain areas and fewer resources in others. You can use your own personal style, and the expertise of yourself and others, to customize your building experience. But it all has to start somewhere, and that somewhere is the vision that becomes the blueprint.

> *Intention creates the blueprint from which*
> *you can build your future.*

Theories abound about how intention works. Many LOA resources refer to intention as a method of "putting your order in" with the Universe, just like you do when you shop from a catalog or an online store or just like you would if you had your very own genie who scrambled to fulfill your every whim. Others suggest that it's a matter of praying for, or requesting, things that mean something to you from your Higher Power, whether you call that power Source, God, Spirit, or some other name. This is where some people get a bit taken aback by either the "groovy" side of the LOA or a particular spiritual element that they don't necessarily resonate with. My own take on intention and the LOA is that, regardless of your belief in a "universal ordering system" or your choice of faith practice, *you* are the key instrument in identifying, setting, and acting on your intention. Pretty much every cultural, faith, or philosophical practice contains a belief in the critical elements of free will and personal accountability, so no matter how you choose to interpret it, you are an integral part of the equation.

> You *are the key instrument in identifying, setting,*
> *and acting on your intention.*

As such, I focus here on your role in setting intention and helping bring it to fruition, and I encourage you to tap into every other aspect of your belief system to help support you in this. Quite simply, your role in setting intention is to know your *preferences*, match them up with an array of infinite *possibilities*, and make a *decision* with certainty about creating that reality in your life. Yep, it's quick, simple, and to the point.

Setting your intention is about the process of sifting through your hopes, dreams, and aspirations, and focusing with clarity on your desires. It's about raising your awareness and applying your focus toward what you *do* want to be, have, and experience in life, in striking contrast to many people's tendency to lament about what they *don't* want. It's about being *present* enough in the current moment to appreciate and celebrate the positive aspects of your life, and about being *receptive* to the signals you are receiving that you want to experience something different in the future. It's allowing yourself to assess the contrast in your life—the things that you find *don't* satisfy you or serve you—so that you can consciously decide what you'd like to turn your attention toward manifesting—additional things that *will* satisfy and serve you.

Setting your intention is decidedly *not* about forgoing your experience of the present in all its glory and challenge in favor of living in the possibility of what the future might bring. On the contrary, it's about soaking in the magic of the here and now, selecting the meaning you want to from your current situation and experiences, while at the same time remaining eager and hopeful about what awaits you just past the horizon. It's appreciating the process of going to school as much as obtaining the degree, as much about enjoying the pregnancy as it is about holding the baby, and as much about traveling to your destination as it is about reaching it. Much of intention is about *choice*—making a choice about where to direct your focus now, a choice about how you interpret what's going on in your life right now, and a choice about how you invest your energy to yield the kinds of outcomes you want in your future.

Intention actually has many different definitions, including its literal interpretation, the state of being "in tension," where *tension* is defined by "the act or action of stretching" or "balancing forces causing extension." This interpretation focuses on the idea that when you set an intention, you are stretching or extending yourself in a new direction, expanding your possibilities and, with them, the promise of positive new outcomes.

Intention is more appropriately referred to, though, as one or more of what I refer to as the Three Ds: desire, determination, and decision. The first idea is that intention is a *desire* to manifest a certain outcome—a matter of truly wanting something to come to pass in your life. Desire includes both *hope* and *eager anticipation*. The second idea is the dictionary classic, which reads that intention is "a *determination* to act in a certain way." This brings an element of both *conviction* and *action* into the picture—a sense that intention isn't just about wishful thinking, it's about creating focus and momentum.

I am most fond, though, of the concept of intention being described as a *decision*, which I first ran across while reading Steve Pavlina's fabulous blog, "Personal Development for Smart People" (see "Resources" for more details). In this definition, intention is steeped in *certainty*—it is a decision to manifest something meaningful in your life. A decision that things will be different in the future. A decision that you will focus your mental and behavioral resources to achieve a worthwhile outcome in your life.

(*Intention is steeped in* certainty—*it is a decision to manifest something meaningful in your life.*)

The reason this is important to spell out is that so many people stumble at several places in their quest for intention. They falter when they choose to believe that they are just pawns in this twisted game called life, subject to the whims of fate or chance or Murphy's Law, rather than believing that they can consciously create their own experience through the way they think and act. And they falter when they simply think about or dream about how things "might be different" in this moment or in the future, rather than *making a discrete decision* about how they want to craft their experience and *proceeding with conviction* in that direction. Sometimes their hesitation is due to fear and uncertainty, sometimes to familiarity and comfort with the status quo, and sometimes to a disbelief that you really *can* shape your experience. In any of these cases, though, *unless you make the decision that things will be different, they most decidedly won't be.*

(*Unless you make the decision that things will be different, they most decidedly won't be.*)

So whether you want to intentionally improve your quality of life as you live with a chronic condition or start a new business, and whether you want to create a more relaxed schedule for yourself or accelerate your education (or any number of other things), it's all about making a *decision* that you'll do that. The decision is powerful, because making a decision implies that you have found your way to a level of certainty that "this shall come to pass" in your life, rather than waffling in the realm of "what-ifs" and "wouldn't it be nices." Sure, it's fun to imagine yourself sporting a great new outfit, lounging on a cushy couch in your redecorated living room, or traveling to an amazing vacation hot spot. But if you want your backside to be parading around in those new jeans, nestled into the cushions of that new couch next to your soul mate, or planted in an airline seat on your way to Belize, you need to do more than just sit around on it, dreaming about what might be. You need to make a *decision* to move your desire from the landscape of your mind into the realm of reality. That process starts with exploring your *preferences* and the *possibilities* associated with what you want to do.

(*You need to make a decision to move your desire from the*
landscape of your mind into the realm of reality.)

Of Preferences and Possibilities

Learning to set your intention is 100 percent linked to your preferences and to the notion that infinite possibilities exist to design your life. It's these preferences and possibilities that hatch your intentions. By exploring and celebrating your *preferences*, you survey your interests and inspirations, those things that give you that little buzz of energy and excitement and make you nod your head in knowing approval. By then examining the *possibilities* for expressing those preferences, you identify your unique path to life satisfaction. It's the combination of your preferences and possibilities that help create your *intentions*, which serve as a powerful personal guidance system—your own compass that stewards you toward the life you were destined to live. Let's start by looking at preferences.

Preferences. Knowing your *preferences* is simply a matter of paying attention to your likes and dislikes, your cravings and aversions, your interests and disinterests. Short of the illegal or immoral (neither of which, I imagine, applies to you), your preferences are not bad. They should not be riddled with judgment. They don't indicate that you are a better or worse person than your parents, your kids, your best friend, or the Joneses. Your preferences are simply—and objectively—yours.

For instance, much to my husband's dismay, I cannot stand lobster. I can't comprehend why anyone could or would or should want to eat it. In fact, I have such an aversion that when he orders it in restaurants, I often have to set up strategically placed little lean-tos in between our place settings using menus and extra tableware so that my gag reflex doesn't get the best of our dinner when he digs in. Along the same lines, he cannot fathom my near-obsessive preoccupation with dark chocolate. You'd think I was chomping on dryer lint for all his hemming and hawing about it. In both cases, it's just a simple *preference* based on our own unique tastes.

The same holds true for other preferences, be they vacation spots or collector cars, professional pursuits or swimming suits. Preferences are all just a matter of knowing what we like, what we appreciate, and what we'd like to experience even more of. Once you know that, setting your intentions and taking inspired action to bring them to fruition become a piece of cake. (Or pie, if that's your preference.)

> *Preferences are all just a matter of knowing what we like, what we appreciate, and what we'd like to experience even more of.*

The hitch is that a lot of people aren't actually *consciously* aware of what their preferences *are*. They've spent enough time living their lives on autopilot that they've lost touch with their genuine desires and interests. So many people operate under beliefs they've had since grade school about how the world is, how people are, and what they should and shouldn't like. They get into a pattern of expecting—and thus perpetuating—the "same old, same old" experiences in their lives so they don't make room for something more enriching or fulfilling. They develop habits that keep them anchored in what *was* or what *is* instead of what *could be*. And then they surround themselves with others who do the same, so they don't have the role models or partners in evolution to help them transform their lives from where they are now to where they want to be.

To illustrate this point, I had a client who complained until she was blue in the face about how her phone rang incessantly, and how, though she hated talking on the phone, she was on calls every night with her father, or friends, or the PTA chair, or even the telemarketers who "were just doing their jobs." She lamented about the time it took away from her family and from her self-care and from just about anything else that would have been more satisfying to her than Super-Gluing a receiver to her ear. When I asked her how long this had been going on, she couldn't even remember because it had just "always been this way."

I suggested that perhaps she could set an intention around how much time and/or energy she wanted to devote to speaking with people on the phone. She said it wouldn't matter what she decided because they would still call and she'd still be "stuck" talking with them. So I recommended that she decide on certain times when she simply wouldn't answer the phone. Her eyes nearly crossed when I said that, and I'm pretty sure she got dizzy when I posed that she could even (gasp) turn off the ringer if she wanted to. She had so distanced herself from her own preferences (a phone-free hour each evening) that it hadn't even occurred to her that she not only had a *choice* about doing this but had the *right* to do it, and that it just might make her both happier and healthier (and perhaps even a more engaged phone conversationalist).

"Oh, but I would never be such a pansy," you say. Maybe not about answering your phone when you don't want to, but what about making time for those workouts you've been talking about for the last four years? Or your tendency to say yes to every new committee that forms at work? What about never getting around to learning Spanish like you want to? Or your resentment over taking on all the household chores when there are other able-bodied family members who could help? Ever think about that long-lost goal to write a book . . . or learn to tango . . . or practice feng shui for cats? How many readers, tango audiences, and unenlightened cats are missing out because you chose *not* to honor these preferences and subsequently chose *not* to set an intention to experience these things in your life?

I'd venture a guess that there are all sorts of preferences you have that you don't recognize or celebrate or cultivate. That may be because they have been obscured by other priorities or by habits or by inattention or whatever, but you do have them. They're in there somewhere. And if they're important enough to you—or intriguing enough—you'll start bringing them up to your conscious level of awareness and start exploring the possibilities associated with them.

Possibilities. When I think about possibilities, I immediately focus in on the notion of the "beginner's mind," a concept central to Zen philosophy. Shunryu Suzuki, founder of the San Francisco Zen Center and author of the book *Zen Mind, Beginner's Mind*, says, "In the beginner's mind there are many possibilities, but in the expert's mind, there are few." Just think about it. When you watch a young child learning to play with something new, he has no idea that a box is meant only to be a container for something else. In the mind of a child, the possibilities for the box's use and enjoyment are endless. It can be a fort, a sailing ship, or a sled. It's a hiding place and a jungle gym. It's a diving platform, a dumping vehicle, a bongo drum, and a dark cave. And that's just in the first ninety seconds. Eventually, almost sadly, kids learn that boxes simply store stuff. But while they have a beginner's mind, not only are their possibilities unlimited, but so is their capacity for joy and adventure. In that constant appreciation of newness exists the perfect framework for building skills and expressing creativity, and the ideal structure for learning and growing. What a gift!

So your ability to effectively explore the possibilities related to your preferences is directly proportional to your ability to maintain a beginner's mind. Dispense with the "been there, done that" mentality, or the "this is the way it's always been" notion. Get rid of the idea that just because you . . . or your friend . . . or some guy in Toledo . . . has tried something that it won't work for you. Avoid getting into the trap that says there are a limited number of ways to do or express or experience anything. Your cardboard box experience could be the process of exploring your unique skills and gifts, opening up an amazing array of opportunities for creative expression. It could be your approach to creating a stunningly, scintillatingly satisfying career. And it could be to the range of options for weaving new avenues for fun and recreation into every day of your life.

> *Your ability to effectively explore the possibilities related to your preferences is directly proportional to your ability to maintain a beginner's mind.*

Possibilities mean that there are a myriad of ways to increase physical activity in your life—it's not just about hitting the treadmill at 5 a.m. every day (unless that's your thing). Possibilities mean that there are many paths to financial freedom that do not mean forgoing every pleasure in life right now (thankfully). Possibilities mean that making time for your friends really can happen, even in the midst of competing priorities and commitments. (Can I get a round of applause on that one?) All it takes is a beginner's mind to *see these possibilities* (or all the others in the life areas that you want to enhance). Then it's time to *set an* intention *to make those possibilities a certainty.*

Cultivating Intentional Certainty

Certainty is the stuff of satisfaction and success. For instance, it's what brings you the meal you want in a restaurant. Imagine going into a restaurant and being completely uncertain about what you wanted, not just at the point of surveying the menu, but at the point of telling the server what to bring you. Imagine waffling back and forth, saying, "Bring me this . . . no . . . that . . . no, I'm not sure if I want that," or suggesting, "I have no idea what I want . . . just pick something and bring it to me." Or what if you knew you weren't that hungry or had food allergies or had a specific dish that you just loved, and you didn't share any of that information with the server? You just said, "I'll have some food, please." Chances are, you'd be mighty disappointed in what you received. You'd wind up with something you likely *didn't* want because you failed to state with certainty what you *did* want.

Certainty is the stuff of satisfaction and success.

Instead, when we go to a restaurant, we give ourselves a bit of time to match our *preferences* up with the *possibilities* on the menu and then we state with *certainty* what we want, such as "Please bring me the Mediterranean pasta and a Caesar salad with dressing on the side." Makes me hungry just thinking about it, to be honest. That's how we know (if the restaurant and server are any good at all) that we'll get what we want. We've made a decision and expressed a certainty that this is what we want brought to us. If we said, "Bring me the Mediterranean pasta *or* the jambalaya *or* the cheese plate *or* whatever you have on hand," you could wind up surprised at best or disappointed (and probably still hungry) at least.

When you make a clear decision and set your intention with conviction, that's when you experience certainty. And that's where the magic happens. There's a fabulous quote from Wolfgang Von Goethe, which reads:

Until one is committed, there is hesitancy, the chance to draw back, always ineffectiveness. Concerning all acts of initiative there is one elementary truth, the ignorance of which kills countless ideas and endless plans: that the moment one definitely commits oneself, then providence moves, too. All sorts of things occur to help one that would never otherwise have occurred. A whole stream of events issues from the decision, raising in one's favor all manner of unforeseen incidents and meetings and material assistance which no man could have dreamed would come his way. Whatever you can do or dream you can, begin it! Boldness has genius, power, and magic in it.

By making the *decision*, you start the intention engine, which powers your progress toward the life of your dreams.

(*By making the decision, you start the intention engine,*
which powers your progress toward the life of your dreams.)

Revving Up the Intention Engine

Recall that setting your intention is dependent on *first* successfully choosing your state. When you choose a productive emotional and physical state, it will unleash phenomenal stores of energy, focus, creativity, and possibility that will supercharge your process of intending. So don't shortchange this step . . . it's not only worth it, it's absolutely essential. Once you have chosen that productive state (and remember it doesn't have to be a "high" energy state . . . just a state that resonates or harmonizes with what it is you want to be experiencing), you start your journey toward uncovering and solidifying your intention. As you now know, the first step involves exploring your *preferences and possibilities*. Then you proceed with *deciding with certainty* what you want, and then you continue by *aligning* yourself emotionally (and vibrationally) with what it is that you want through a series of techniques that you can customize.

The process of exploring your preferences and possibilities is the work of both the observer and the dreamer in you. The *observer* pays attention to how things are right now in your life and analyzes that situation (sometimes consciously, sometimes subconsciously) based on how it makes you feel. The *dreamer* pays attention to your notion of what the "ideal life" would feel like to you—what you would experience, have, do, be, and how you would feel as a result of that. Then, you examine the contrast between your reality and your notion of the ideal to determine what could be different and what you want to do about it.

(*The process of exploring your preferences and possibilities is the work of both the observer and the dreamer in you.*)

It's kind of like the process used by skilled movie reviewers, who start with an idea of what the "ideal" film experience is—from plot and direction to acting and cinematography, and a host of other considerations. Then, they measure their *actual* experience against that notion of what is *ideal* by their standards and generate a report of their findings: "These things were stellar, these things were average, and these things could use a bit of work." Certainly, every movie critic has his or her personal preferences (a unique perspective on what is "ideal"), just as we all have our own interpretation of what is ideal in our life. That's what makes both movies—and life—so very interesting. But the movie critic's job ends with their rating. Your work continues.

Once you make that comparison between the *reality* of your current circumstance and the *idea* of what you would like to be experiencing, you have several important tasks. First, you turn your attention briefly toward the elements of your life that are *not* as you would like them to be, objectively *assess* them to gain clarity, and *immediately* shift your focus to the alternative feelings and experiences you would *like* to be experiencing. Get yourself into a creative space to truly envision how you want things to be in the future (whether that future is in thirty seconds or in thirty years). Next, you *make a decision* that you will focus your attention and energy on experiencing this new reality in your future. This decision comes from a sense of hope and eagerness, and is centered in *certainty* that what you want is not only *possible*, not only *probable*, but *inevitable*. Finally, you align yourself with the state you want to be experiencing with those new desires by getting yourself in the "feeling place" of already having them. Focusing on the feeling of having them effectively trains your mind to help draw what you want into your experience. Yes, it's that simple. But the question I always hear is "But does it really work . . . and if so, how?"

This decision comes from a sense of hope and
eagerness, and is centered in certainty *that what*
you want is not only possible, *not only*
probable, *but* inevitable.

Yes, It Works . . . And How!

I always like proof. That's why I love the fact that there are a variety of research projects that have shown that setting an intention really does work to influence outcomes. In her book *The Intention Experiment*, Lynne McTaggart has collected an outstanding array of research that shows how powerfully intention impacts everything from machines to bacteria to cells, and from athletic performance to medical healing to crime rates. Following are a few highlights of these study findings.

Studies have shown that people can intentionally influence the outcome of machines programmed to generate random numbers, making their output more orderly. While it may not be strong enough of an influence for you to grab the mortgage money and head to Vegas to make slot machine history, it is a real—and measurable—outcome of intentional thinking.

Other studies have shown that test subjects were able to influence the mutation of *E. coli* cultures by focusing positive or negative intentions for the samples to mutate. The study showed higher than normal mutation in samples that had received the positive intention to mutate and lower than normal mutation in those that had received the negative intention (not to mutate). Similarly, an interesting study of an American physician and healer found that he was able to influence the growth rate of cancer cells in test tubes. The study looked at several ways of sending intention, among them making a "request" that the cells return to a natural rate of growth and visualizing fewer cancer cells in the sample. The results were fascinating, showing significant reductions in the number of cancer cells of between 21 and 40 percent for several of the methods of intention.

Okay, so intentionally influencing random-number machines and *E. coli* and cancerous cells might make for an engaging party trick, but maybe it's not compelling enough for you. In that case, let's look at examples of the impact of focused intention on *human* outcomes. Many studies have shown that elite athletes who mentally rehearse their performance perform better than those who don't, a finding that has been validated by the National Academy of Sciences. Various research involving skiers, boxers, football players, champion rowers, and a variety of other athletes show that they rely on "highly detailed internal images and run-throughs" to enhance their performance. These athletes rehearse their feelings— their elation and emotional response to winning—and they engage all their senses in the mental rehearsal, particularly the sense of "feel" or kinesthetic sensations. McTaggart notes that "the most important aspect of the intention is to rehearse the victory; rehearsal appears to help secure victory."

Other studies have found that by intentionally focusing in the mind, you can impact the body's responses. Skiers who mentally rehearsed their downhill runs had brain/body scans showing that the brain sends the same electrical impulses to the body whether they were mentally *rehearsing* the run or actually *executing* it. This finding supports the statement that underlies all this intentional work on the personal level . . . *the mind produces the same activity regardless of whether you are recalling something, observing something, or vividly imagining something.*

The mind produces the same activity regardless of whether you are recalling something, observing something, or vividly imagining something.

Evidence suggests that intention is more than just channeling energy or guiding muscle twitches—intention actually impacts *results*, too. In several studies, participants who trained in a gym increased their muscle strength by 30 percent, while their counterparts who only mentally rehearsed their training increased strength by almost half as much. While this doesn't promise you a visualization-induced hard body, it does suggest that the mind can effect real and measurable changes in the body. Similarly, highly detailed visualization processes have favorably impacted a host of health issues, including chronic conditions, pain management, surgical outcomes, and side effects from cancer treatments (among others).

Even the *unconscious* forming of an intention, as seen in the outcomes associated with the placebo effect, show remarkable results. The placebo effect occurs when a patient's *belief* in a treatment yields similar effects on their body or disease process even if it's not an active treatment, as in the instance of patients getting a sugar pill rather than an active medicine. Studies have shown that heart patients taking a placebo had the same survival rates as those taking a specific heart drug (provided they believed it would work and actually took the prescribed regimen). Parkinson's patients showed increased levels of naturally occurring dopamine in their brains upon being told that they had been given dopamine. And in still another study, patients suffering with arthritis of the knee experienced similar improvements in pain and function, regardless of whether they had actually had knee surgery or had simply undergone anesthesia and an incision in the knee with no real surgery. In fact, the placebo group had better outcomes than some patients who had actually had the surgery. These examples show that the mind can be as powerful a source of healing at times—if not more so—than interventions occurring outside of the body. In short, expectations often precede experience.

(*Expectations often precede experience.*)

And what about the impact of collective intention—groups of people focusing intention on a social or community issue? One of the most interesting outcomes in this arena comes from the results of more than twenty studies that have shown the positive effect that intentional meditation can have on reducing conflict and violence. The outcome, known as the Maharishi Effect of Transcendental Meditation, showed that when a certain threshold of people meditated in a given area, it significantly reduced crime rates. For example, one study showed a 22 percent reduction in crime rates and an 89 percent reduction in crime trends in a specific city during the period of the intervention.

These examples of the powerful effects of intention reflect only a handful of the studies suggesting that when you direct your focus toward an intended outcome, you can actually influence it. In my mind, this evidence provides a solid foundation not only to *believe,* but to *act* as if intention is one of the most powerful processes you can use for transforming your life. Research is certainly convincing, but real-life stories are even more compelling, as you can see from some of the following tales that illustrate the power of intention.

More Examples Abound: The Power of Intention

Child's Day. Ellen and Jason had spent years trying to conceive a child, first naturally, then using fertility drugs, and then through in-vitro fertilization, all to no avail. They then spent several more years hoping for a successful adoption (including several cases where they had been parenting a child who was subsequently returned to the birth parents). They were disappointed and disillusioned, but after a period of time, they made the choice to release all their disappointment and hurt around the previous experiences and focus *exclusively* on their desire to bring the child they were meant to parent into their lives at exactly the right moment. After all those years of trying every option they could, Ellen declared to a group of her new friends one evening, "My only intention for this year is to become a parent at exactly the right time." Less than twenty-four hours later, without advance notice, she received a call from the adoption agency that their child was on the way. The adoption went smoothly and they are now, two years later, the happy, satisfied parents of not just one, but two incredible boys. They attribute this outcome to the clarity of intention and the positive energy they projected.

It's All in the List. Jennifer and Elizabeth are women from different countries with similar stories of long-term relationships that left them disillusioned, dissatisfied, and nearly despondent. After recovering from their disappointment, both of them went through an exercise of journaling about the *exact* characteristics of their ideal partners, listing everything from personality traits, to interests, to physical characteristics. For one, within two weeks she fell in love with her now husband of ten years. For the other, within several months she met and married the man of her dreams and they are happier today than they were when they met eight years ago. Both women stumbled across their journal entries some time after they married and found, to their astonishment, that their respective partners met every single quality on their list of desired traits in an ideal partner. Both women vividly detailed their intention and then "let it go," realizing only after they met their mates that their intention had yielded such powerful results.

The Check's in the Mail. After first learning about the principles of the Law of Attraction, Trent, a psychologist, decided he would set an intention to find money in his personal mailbox one morning even though he wasn't expecting anything of the sort. He centered himself in an appreciative, energetic state and went to check the mail. To his amazement, there sat a check for a significant refund of a premium he had paid for a service several years prior. He had no idea that the service had been overpaid, nor that he was due a refund, and yet the check landed in his mailbox on the very day that he intended to receive one. He had never tried such an experiment before and hadn't received a check like that in his recent memory until the day he set a playful, but conscious, intention to receive one.

Home Free. Claire, a midlife woman who had recently undergone successful cancer treatment, set an intention to focus on what was truly important to her. She decided to downsize her life by selling her home and moving into a condominium. She hadn't had an opportunity to act on this desire to put her home on the market, but focused on the joy and energy she felt simply about having made the decision, while mentally envisioning a successful transition into her downsized existence. Within days, there was an unexpected knock at the door by a couple who indicated that they loved the neighborhood and had fallen in love with her home. They stopped on the off chance that she would consider an unsolicited offer on her home even though it wasn't on the market. She is now happily living in her new condo, thrilled with the ideal result that her intention produced.

Chai Factor. Tanya, a photographer with a thriving business, set about her daily schedule in the mood for a chai latte. She began her day of appointments and found that her schedule was too full and wouldn't allow her to stop long enough to indulge her craving, so she decided to simply "go there in her mind." She vividly imagined savoring the scent, the heat, and the taste of her favorite treat. She drove from meeting to meeting enjoying the pleasure of her imaginary chai. She returned to her home office later that day to find a warm chai latte sitting on her porch with a note from her neighbor, a friend, who wanted to do something nice for her that day by delivering her favorite indulgence to her doorstep. Her intention yielded a kind intervention from a friend.

These are just a few of the examples that demonstrate the power of setting an intention. It's like creating your own little gravitational pull that attracts favorable outcomes to you—or not so favorable, if you're not careful! Part Two will provide you with a variety of strategies to clearly define your intention. In the meantime, while it's true that *intention* sets the stage for bringing all sorts of good things into your experience, it's a matter of taking *inspired action* that helps set the whole machine into motion. That's what we'll be focusing on next.

CHAPTER FOUR

Your Next Best Step:
Taking Inspired Action

Straddling the Snare

For wildly elusive reasons, I have this obsessive desire to learn to play the drums. I'm not exactly sure why, since the drums are the single *least* likely instrument I would be drawn to. I am not rhythmic in the least, with the exception of my childhood passion for classical ballet. Even so, somehow, the notion of a ballerina banging out a sweaty drum solo isn't an image that's easy on the brain, though I guess it would be quite a sight to see a straitlaced dancer, all tutus and toe shoes, jamming with some rock band.

One day, as I was focusing on some of my personal Law of Attraction practices, I decided it was time to refine my "dream boards," which consist of pictures and phrases of the key experiences and things I want to have in my life. They cover everything from how I want to be as a person, to where I want to travel, to my professional and philanthropic efforts. Health, wealth, happiness, service, success . . . you name it, it's there on my boards.

In any case, the key to this dream/vision board process is to include vivid images of how you want your life to be so that your mind begins working on your behalf—both consciously and sub-consciously—to help manifest those desires. It basically helps anchor your mind to a visual image and to the "feeling" of having what you desire, which increases the likelihood you will achieve it. As I've mentioned, visualizing helps you attract what you want by activating a part of your brain called the reticular activating system (RAS). The RAS opens your eyes and your mind to opportunities, resources, and ideas that help you realize your goals more easily and quickly than you could ever imagine.

One thing that dawned on me, though, was that I was missing a picture of this long-held dream to play the drums. Right around the time I realized this, I attended my friend Alison's wedding. The band had some technical difficulties, so while everyone else was selflessly lending a helping hand to get the music up and running, I jumped at the chance to sit down at the vacated drums and have my picture taken for my dream board.

I sauntered up to the drummer, whom I'm sure was poised to hear some suggestion about the electrical problems or a compliment about her playing. Instead, what she faced was something akin to a kindergartner accosting a Disney character for a photo op when I said, "Can I have my picture taken with your drums because I want to be a drummer when I grow up." She raised an eyebrow, certain, I'm sure, that I was floating on my very own champagne cloud, and simply said, "Of course, but be sure you straddle the snare so you really look like you know what you're doing."

Hmmmm. I didn't really know what a snare was and I certainly had never been invited to straddle one. It felt a bit risqué, a bit sassy, perhaps illicit in some way. I wasn't altogether certain that good Lutheran girls (or even moderately not-too-terribly-bad Lutheran girls like myself) straddled things like snares. She saw my trepidation, led me over to the drum set, and showed me how to sit. She positioned my hands with the sticks, and told me to mug for the camera. And voilà, thanks to the beauty of digital cameras, I had immediate visual proof that percussion would be more promising in my future.

After viewing the picture, I simply *knew* that it would lead to my learning to drum sooner rather than later—after all, I had chosen a great, energetic state and had set a clear intention, with visualization tools and everything. I could feel it coming. So I began imagining what it would be like to catalog the journey from hatching this goal to its realization.

I recalled that my first interest was associated with the rousing song "Bang on the Drum": "I don't want to work, I just want to bang on the drum all day . . ." Then, I traced that fledgling interest forward to the long-standing bantering between my husband and me about the possibilities of learning to play the drums so that I could accompany him as an accordion player. We had always joked that by doing so, we would be the life of the party wherever we went, the center stage for family events, and (no doubt) the bane of our children's existence. I mean, who can resist grinning and toe tapping in the presence of a really good polka?

Now, the likelihood of my husband's playing the accordion is even more of a stretch of the imagination than my playing the drums. In fact, I'm convinced that, aside from the amusement factor inherent in accordion playing in general, his real motive is to be a perennial invitee to everyone's Oktoberfest celebrations owing to his propensity for enjoying a good German brewski on occasion. But back to the story at hand. The fact of the matter is that Michael is the unlikeliest of accordion players and I am the unlikeliest of drummers, which makes it even more blissfully entertaining to imagine our little polka band of the future.

As I visualized, rather than asking "How will I make this happen?" or focusing on things like time constraints, the fact that I have no detectable musical ability whatsoever, or questions about the current market for polka bands, I just pictured the image of me straddling the snare and smiled. My mind bounced among a few famous drum solos until I settled on the song "Wipeout," which has one of those catchy solos that really sticks with you.

All of a sudden, I felt this rush of excitement when I realized that, at a conference earlier that year, I had met Rick, a drummer who played with The Surfaris, the band best known for their song "Wipeout." How very convenient, don't you think? I remembered what a kind person he was and started wondering what it might be like to learn how to play a drum solo from a drummer of his talent. Okay, I'm not necessarily ambitious enough to attempt "Wipeout" at the offset, but I figured any drum solo would do. My gut said to give it a go and explore the possibility.

So I jumped at the chance and fired off a quick email to him, telling him about my goal and asking if he might be willing to teach me a drum solo. Much to my delight, he responded to my request with an immediate and gracious "yes," and told me how to get started so I'd be familiar with the drums before we met. Then, it would just be a matter of the logistics of meeting up in the same city to make it happen. I was giddy and filled with awe. I mean, I had been casually talking about playing the drums for years, but it wasn't until I created a specific *intention* and then took swift *action* that opportunities beyond my wildest imagination presented themselves. Who knew that, simply by straddling the snare, I'd be well on my way to knowing how to use it? That's what this chapter is all about . . . taking inspired *action*—swift and certain—to yield *results* in your life.

Cue the Lights . . . and . . . Action!

Intention is similar to *deciding* to turn on the light in a darkened room. You can think about how nice it would be to have light in the room, imagine how it would help you see or do what you want, and even plan to make it a reality. But until you flip the switch, you'll probably remain drenched in darkness until someone . . . or something . . . makes a move on your behalf. Since waiting for some other force to turn on the lights—or to transform our lives— is a recipe for a life of wishful thinking and waiting, I'm all for taking inspired action on your own accord.

One of the most common criticisms of recent LOA literature and movies is that people mistakenly believe the LOA suggests that you simply (and only) "think happy thoughts and wait for good things to happen." This reminds me of a cartoon I once saw of a professor solving a math problem on a chalkboard. The problem starts out with a slew of cryptic symbols hinting toward obvious confusion and intellectual mayhem. Then, somewhere in the middle of the board you see a huge blank space with the caption "a miracle happens," followed by a neat and tidy solution at the end of the chalkboard.

While it would be nice to think that this type of approach to life change would be not only *possible* but actually *commonplace*, we all know that in truth, it's *not*. Furthermore, it's *not* how the LOA and all its related bodies of science and practice actually work. Real and lasting change and success always emerge by *first* choosing your state and *then* setting a clear intention for what you want to achieve. They require something more, though, to actually yield results. That "something more" is *inspired action*.

This isn't meant to pooh-pooh serendipity or synchronicity or any of those wonderful things (I'm actually a big fan of them all).

What it does mean, however, is that in order to move forward in life, you need to *take inspired action consistently*. Sometimes seemingly minor and sometimes momentous, but always the same—action. Now, this action might be in the form of changing your perspective, seeking out resources, connecting with someone, or rolling up your sleeves and putting some muscle into crafting change. But it always means "to act."

> *In order to move forward in life, you need to take inspired action consistently.*

We need to distinguish, though, between the concept of "frenetic activity" and the concept of "inspired action." So many people are caught in the trap of pressured, frantic activity in their lives that yields no real results. They adopt an "at all costs" attitude that actually *compromises* the success they're after, because it isn't attached to their values and their quality of life, much less to the powerful vision of the intention they've set. This is what results from a common human tendency toward pressure rather than progress, straining rather than strategizing, and flailing rather than flowing. In short, it's a recipe for unproductive and dissatisfying activity that typically yields unproductive and dissatisfying results. The alternative is not only much more *pleasant*, but also far more *productive*. That alternative is *inspired action*.

> *We need to distinguish between the concept of "frenetic activity" and the concept of "inspired action."*

A Breath of Fresh Air

What is inspired action? It's intuitively identifying your "next best step" and moving forward with a learning mind and committed heart. It's coming from a place of silence that yields an inner knowing of your options, combined artfully with passion and conviction. It's charting a steady course by taking one additional stride forward at a time.

The idea of inspired action comes from the concept of *inspiration*, which is derived from the word *inspire*. The Latin root for *inspire* is *inspirare*, which means "to breathe in." Another definition includes, "to exert an animating or enlivening experience." Inspired action embodies what both of these definitions suggest— an ease, and a simplicity in identifying your "next best step." When we breathe in, it's a natural process that doesn't require force (okay, with the exception of a few health issues or an over-the-top workout). But in general, we don't have to orchestrate it, plan it, or overthink it. We just do it. And the idea of animating or enlivening suggests an energy, a rising to the occasion, that comes from feeling moved toward something—drawn toward something (as opposed to pushed toward something clawing, kicking, and screaming).

Inspired action is, at its core, an intuitive "knowing" of your *next best step*. It's *not* a matter of knowing *every* step between where you are now and where you want to be, and though it's a plus, it's *not* even a matter of knowing an *array* of *many* steps that could move you forward. It's only about seeking out your *next best step*. Your next best step is the one step forward that you feel intrinsically compelled to take. It's only one step—just like stepping out onto the first of a path of stones that will help you cross a stream—and it's the best one—the one that feels not only logical, but also natural, joyously powerful . . . and inevitable.

(*Inspired action is, at its core, an intuitive "knowing" of your*
next best step. It's not a matter of knowing every step
between where you are now and where you want to be.)

Don't get the idea that I'm saying that inspired action is always easy. Because it's not. Taking action isn't always *easy,* but it is always *simple.* Yes, at times it requires a significant amount of sweat equity (thus the old saying that "success is equal parts inspiration and perspiration"). Sometimes it involves a marathon deadline, or a process of building—and using—more mental and physical muscles than you care to at times. But it always originates from a very simple process performed in a very quiet space. It presents itself when you calm the mind enough to focus in on that spark of insight, that gut instinct, that tells you which direction to go. Then, it's your role to make a *choice* to act and to get up and *do something.* Most of the time, the process of taking inspired action yields quiet insight rather than screaming innovation (though I wouldn't turn down either of them). That's why you need to be prepared to listen for it and to act with speed and sureness before you lose either the message or the motivation.

(*Taking action isn't always* easy, *but it is always* simple.)

The Art of Thinking Big and Acting Small

Inspired action is based, in part, on the tradition of the Japanese concept of Kaizen, which is the foundation for the practice of "continuous improvement." Hold on . . . I'm not going to lapse into the corporate platitudes on "continuous quality improvement." I'm just using the concept of Kaizen in its truest sense. The Japanese definition of the word *Kaizen* is "change for the better." All buzzwords and paradigm shifts and "thinking outside the box" aside, Kaizen is really all about "the art of thinking big and acting small."

In his fabulous book, *One Small Step Can Change Your Life: The Kaizen Way*, Robert Maurer suggests that we "meet life's constant demands for change by seeking out continual—but always small—improvement." This philosophy is rooted in the two-thousand-year-old wisdom of the Tao Te Ching: "The journey of a thousand miles begins with a single step." Kaizen is the art of making great and lasting change through small, steady increments. According to Maurer, this involves, among other things, asking small questions that help inspire creativity; thinking small thoughts that help you build new skills and habits to support your success; taking small steps that guarantee success and progress; solving small problems, even in the midst of bigger ones; treating yourself to small rewards that spark additional momentum; and recognizing small but crucial moments that others tend to ignore.

> *Kaizen is the art of making great and lasting change through small, steady increments.*

Kaizen is all about "learning by doing," rather than assuming that you need to know the *best* route to a goal or the *right* solution to a challenge before you ever jump into it—that's why it's perfectly aligned with the idea of taking inspired action. One of the key principles of Kaizen is to eliminate waste, which essentially means activities that add cost without adding value. This is important, because so many people spend an inordinate amount of time just doing things, anything, often too many things too quickly and with too little intention. They mistake mindless activity for purposeful action. The opposite of what I call this "calamity of activity" is the idea of inspired action. Thoughtful choices followed by small steps lead to big results.

> *Thoughtful choices followed by small steps*
> *lead to big results.*

Small steps are less intimidating than sweeping changes, although they often lead to a chain reaction that produces them. They're also much more manageable and more often than not more enjoyable than huge leaps. When a couple decides to have a child together, the Kaizen approach could yield a much more relaxed (and thankfully pleasurable) experience than a radical "shift your life and focus every ounce of your anxious energy on getting pregnant." Losing weight can be much more appealing when it's a matter of making one modest shift at a time in how you think, how you behave, and your environment, rather than relying on the New Year's Resolution approach to radical deprivation. Launching a new business endeavor can come together much more readily and joyfully when you allow yourself to identify and act on the most powerful possibilities and opportunities rather than thinking you need to do everything at once.

I had a client who had tried just about everything she could to lose weight and keep it off. She tried every diet imaginable and every attempt left her even more discouraged and even heavier than before. She decided to use the inspired action approach to losing weight and relied on the Kaizen strategy of asking herself, "What one small thing can I do today that will make a difference in my weight and well-being?" As she asked this question each day, she started being "led" toward small behavior and thought changes that started making a big difference in her food intake and her level of physical activity. She started by eating a healthy breakfast most days, which changed her appetite for the day and gave her more energy. Then, at one point, she felt moved to create a vision board of her idea of ideal weight and well-being, which she reviewed each day. She started with small bouts of activity—taking the stairs instead of the elevator and eventually moving up to ten minutes of walking each day.

The magic happened because she simply just kept asking the question "What one small thing can I do?" and each time an answer energized her (or at least didn't paralyze her!), she took action—purposefully and immediately. Before long she had transformed both her physical body and her emotional outlook without ever feeling deprived or overwhelmed (or any of those negative emotions that can tend to keep us from doing what we want to do). Because she set herself up for both consistent change and near-certain success, she built momentum quickly and was able not only to lose the weight she wanted to, but also to thoroughly enjoy the process. Now there's a perk you don't often hear about in the realm of weight loss!

How to Take Inspired Action

Inspired action emerges from a series of five simple steps, including: quieting your mind, asking simple questions about next steps, taking initiative in the form of immediate action, gaining momentum with consistent progress, and reflecting on and building on that progress to sustain continued success. We'll look at each of these steps here, and then introduce strategies for taking Inspired Action in Part Two.

Quieting Your Mind. Inspired action first requires getting yourself to a place of *silence*. The goal is to quiet the "monkey mind" that is ever-present in our modern society long enough to allow creative thought to filter out of the frenzy and information overload. This can come from many angles, including various forms of meditation, focused breath work, the active "purging" of extra information and concerns, directed attention toward a repetitive or rhythmic activity, or using resources such as audio programs that help relax the body and create favorable brainwaves for relaxation and creativity. Silence is the space from which creativity flows. Have you ever noticed that your very best ideas, insights, and problem-solving solutions *always* seem to come during times when you are *not* actively thinking about something? We tend to solve the world's problems (or at least our own!) in the shower, on the commute, while walking the dog, chopping vegetables, or watching the sunset. When your mind has gently released all its preoccupations, it gives you a blank slate on which to write your next best step. Your insights flow from this place of peace and quiet.

> Silence is the space from which creativity flows.

Asking Simple Questions. The next step in taking inspired action is to ask yourself very simply but sometimes repeatedly, "*What is my next best step?*" and then allow the answer to unfold rather than forcing a solution or direction. This is really the process of planting the seed for your intuitive self to offer up creative solutions and insights. By asking the question and allowing the answer to present itself without any "forcing," you set yourself up for a smooth, at times seemingly effortless, presentation of the very best path you can take to achieve your desires. This notion is akin to a wonderful analogy shared in the Abraham-Hicks "Art of Allowing" workshops (see "Resources" for more details), which suggests that there is a stream of well-being and forward momentum that you can tap into, regardless of the endeavor you're working on. It's a matter of allowing yourself to flow *with* the current of the river, rather than paddling upstream all the time. So much of our lives is spent *striving* against so many natural forces that it can feel like a tremendous relief—and equally productive—to simply allow the journey, and the scenery, and the experience itself to unfold. One caution, though: Be careful to choose the right river leading in *the direction you want to go, with an eye on your destination at all times!*

Taking Initiative. Third, inspired action relies on your *initiative*—taking that first critical step to act, and acting *now*. This helps avoid the perpetual duel between a great idea and our tendency to shoot it down with every reason that it *can't* work, *hasn't* worked in the past, *won't* work this time, or *didn't* work for your cousin Joe. People seem to get caught up in the notion that action has to be momentous and revolutionary at best, strenuous and arduous at worst. This couldn't be farther from the truth. Sure, *sometimes* we're ready for monumental change—for innovation that will transform our situation right now and forever. In those cases, that type of change will *still* feel like it is the next best step—the step that you couldn't imagine *not* taking—the step that you feel so internally inspired to take that the fear or the prospect of hard work or the idea that it's big simply dissipates into the process of experiencing it. This is a good thing . . . an exciting thing founded in eager anticipation of what's to come, rather than dread and disillusionment about what it's going to take to get there.

(People seem to get caught up in the notion that action has
to be momentous and revolutionary at best, strenuous and
arduous at worst. This couldn't be farther from the truth.)

This is an example of a state called Flow, which Mihaly Csik-menthalyi, author of *Finding Flow*, characterizes as moments of complete immersion in a worthwhile endeavor. Many people recall moments like these as some of the best times of their lives, even though they can require a significant amount of focus, skill, and hard work. States like these yield phenomenal results, both in terms of tangible progress and in terms of psychological capital, and they actually feel both motivating and natural, despite their intensity.

Yet this type of immersion in change isn't the *only* type of inspired action that exists. There's also a much subtler form of action that creates results just as outstanding, and that's the idea of small, immediate steps in the direction you want to move. By taking small steps on a continuous basis, you minimize two things: the chance that fear will overcome you and the possibility that a task will seem so daunting that it will rob you of your resolve. It requires taking those next best steps, though, when the idea and the opportunity present themselves, because otherwise it can be easy to get into the mind-set of thinking it won't really make a difference or it's not worth it. On the contrary, some of the smallest steps can set the stage for the most exquisite success in life. The small step of picking up a particular book can change your whole outlook on something. The small step of meeting someone new can yield the most powerful business relationship you could ever imagine. The small step of creating a new habit can release energy and creativity in your life to change the world.

(*By taking small steps on a continuous basis, you minimize*
the chance that fear will overcome you, or that the idea
that a task seems daunting will rob you of your resolve.)

Gaining Momentum. The fourth component of inspired action is to build *momentum* through consistent (but smart!) action that yields consistent (no matter how small!) results. It's the feedback from consistent action—the celebration of successes, the new insights it produces, and the general energy it creates—that yields more desire and more forward motion. Back to science class for a minute or two. Newton's First Law of Motion (also known as the Law of Inertia) states that, "An object at rest tends to stay at rest and an object in motion tends to stay in motion with the same speed and in the same direction unless acted upon by an unbalanced force." Whew. What this means is that if you want to go from *rest* (or the status quo) to *action*, you'll need to provide enough *force* (in the form of ideas, inspiration, aversion to pain, desire for pleasure, or a host of other things) to get you to a state of *motion*. Often, this requires only small steps that start a cycle of action. Then, you need to keep those small actions going consistently to avoid allowing yourself to have the unbalanced force of fear, uncertainty, or the idea that change is hard stop you in your tracks and take you back to a state of rest again. When you want to get a train or boat moving, it takes a flurry of small steps and consistent energy to get such a massive thing to budge. But once it's in motion, its mass and momentum keep it going. The same holds true for you, only your mass is related to the passion behind your intention, and your momentum comes from small, significant steps in the right direction.

Reflecting on Progress. Finally, inspired action works best when you integrate reflection and evaluation into your process so that you are constantly analyzing your trajectory toward your desired outcomes and correcting your course as needed. This is where your learning mind comes into play, and you can actually be playful about monitoring success and progress, troubleshooting challenges, and problem solving as needed. This process of reflection and evaluation is best used when it includes both an objective and a subjective approach to learning.

The *objective* approach is what I think of as the "autopilot analogy." When you put a plane on autopilot, it is programmed to head toward the destination, but for most of the trip, the plane is actually performing course corrections. Although it appears to be, the plane is almost never directly on target. It simply (and yes, objectively) corrects itself when the wind changes or when it veers slightly off course. The plane doesn't go through a process of judging and scolding itself for not being on track all the time—it simply notices when something is not quite right and immediately makes a change to right itself.

The *subjective* approach to learning is a matter of paying close attention to the *progress* that's being made on your journey. It involves cataloging the milestones or benchmarks on the way from here to there, paying attention to the evidence that you are, indeed, moving toward where you want to be. Why is this so important? Primarily because we are goal-oriented beings who thrive on progress. This is why scientists have proven that we actually experience an endorphin "rush" when we check something off our to-do list. This explains why, when you realize that something you've just done isn't on your list, you actually take the time to add it just so that you'll have the opportunity to cross it off. Sound familiar? Being goal-oriented is also why we have specific notions of how much we want to earn, what size we want to wear, and what type of home we want to live in. It's why sports have such a huge fan base, why quilters finish their projects, and why there's something just way too cool about seeing those shelves you finally hung in the garage or that exquisite rose bloom on the bush you tended all year. We like to see *results*. We like to see *progress*. We instinctively know that *goals matter*. So, the subjective approach to the learning mind involves not just *noticing* progress, but also *celebrating* it and *building* on it. Indeed, it's often during the process of cataloging evidence that we're moving toward a goal that we hatch our next idea for inspired action.

> *We are goal-oriented beings . . . We like to see* results. *We like to see* progress. *We instinctively know that* goals matter.

I love the idea of focusing at the same time on how far you've come and on the vivid imagery of where you want to be. Both of these targets are empowering targets—one reminds you of your *success* and creates the *momentum* for more of the same. The other keeps you *inspired* to continue moving *forward*. It's when we focus on the *gap* between where we are now and where we want to be that we become lost in that void of uncertainty and fear. Tightrope artists would tumble from the wire if they focused on the space between themselves and the platform. Instead, they keep their eye on the platform itself and take one thoughtful step at a time until they make it to the other side. This strategy can work for you, too.

Embrace the Gray

In my opinion, inspired action also requires that you view challenging experiences and outcomes from a stance of interest and discovery, rather than one of judgment or disappointment. It's about choosing the meaning you want to take from any experience and using that meaning to define your next best step. This allows you to learn and grow from everything you do without getting hung up on the notion of failure. So often, people get caught up in an all-or-nothing or black-or-white mentality that their outcomes are either an unprecedented success in the way they first envisioned they would be, or they are an utter, dismal failure. The learning mind knows that all or nothing doesn't exist . . . there are a myriad of progress points along the journey. And black or white typically doesn't exist either . . . there are exquisite shades of gray in every situation. So I always tell my clients, "Embrace the gray!"

Inspired action also requires that you view challenging experiences and outcomes from a stance of interest and discovery, rather than one of judgment or disappointment.

Nothing is good or bad until you define it that way, and nothing is a true failure unless you give up. So long as you are focusing on the progress you've made and what you can learn from any setback, and so long as you continue moving forward, you're still on your way to manifesting your dreams. So when in doubt, reframe every setback, challenge, or perceived failure into an opportunity to learn about what has and hasn't worked up to this point, and what small changes you want to make to correct your course.

Lee Iacocca, former chairman of the Chrysler Corporation, offered some outstanding insight on this topic when he said:

So what do we do? Anything—something. So long as we don't just sit there. If we screw it up, start over. Try something else. If we wait until we've satisfied all the uncertainties, it may be too late.

His words seem so commonsense and at the same time profound. They are all about what it means to take inspired action and to continue moving forward, even in the face of setbacks or disappointments. It's movement that creates momentum, and momentum that creates magic.

> *It's movement that creates momentum, and momentum that creates magic.*

Release Your Resistance

Try this little party trick. Face a partner and make a gentle fist—not a threatening one! Ask your partner to do the same. Place your fist against her fist, and without saying a word, begin gently pressing against her fist. You'll notice that she will immediately begin pressing back against your fist. Don't turn it into a shoving match; just ask the person, "Why are you pushing against me?" Inevitably she'll respond, "Because *you* are pushing against *me*." This example illustrates the point that we seem naturally inclined to resist forces that press against us. Without thinking, and without consciously choosing, we respond in-kind to pressure, applying pressure right back, whether it's in a contrived situation like this one or when it has to do with negative emotions, disappointments, or challenges. When something pushes against us, we push back, whether it's needed or not (and whether we'd be better off simply to shrug off the pressure and allow it to dissipate). This can be very counterproductive to allowing the flow of abundance into our lives.

During a recent conversation, Bob Doyle, creator of the *Wealth Beyond Reason* program and one of the teachers featured on *The Secret*, mentioned to me that if there is one thing that tends to get in the way of people's success using the LOA, it is *resistance to allowing what they want to naturally unfold in their lives.* That resistance can be in the form of having limiting beliefs about whether or not they can achieve a goal, or around negative emotional patterns, or even about the notion of feeling deserving enough to experience what you want. I couldn't agree more. In Part Two, we will be exploring a variety of ways to release resistance, although it's also important to keep some of the following reminders in front of you at all times.

For the greatest success with the LOA, your role is *not* to force progress or strive for perfection. And it is *not* to have a predetermined path toward what you want to manifest. It is simply to choose the most productive state that will help you be in resonance with what you want, to set your intention with utter clarity and certainty about what you want, and then to take your next best step—inspired action—to move a tiny bit closer to that reality. It is critical to then *detach* yourself from thinking that it needs to unfold in a *certain* way, on a *specific* time line, or to your *exact* specifications. This helps preserve your creativity and it maximizes the possible ways that you can get from where you are to where you want to be (all while enjoying both your now and your journey). And finally, it is just as important to release those negative thought patterns or limiting beliefs that tend to keep you where you are now. The key is that you have to be willing to shift your focus from what you've seen in the past and what is in front of you now if you want to see the beautiful vistas that are waiting for you just beyond the horizon.

You have to be willing to shift your focus from what
(*you've seen in the past and what is in front of you now if*)
you want to see the beautiful vistas that are waiting for
you just beyond the horizon.

Still More Examples Abound: The Power of Inspired Action

Now that you understand the basics about taking inspired action, we'll look at a few stories of how it has helped create desired outcomes for others.

Business Basics. Brooke and Chris, business partners in a technology firm, went through a strategic planning process to hone their vision and align their work with what they were truly passionate about. They made a tough decision—to let go of a highly lucrative but unfulfilling contract that had been sustaining their profit margins for some time. At the same time, they wanted to markedly increase their income. They set a clear intention—not only to replace the income from the former contract with work they felt more passionate about, but also to double their gross revenues in the coming year—a tall order! They stepped back, surveyed their current situation, took some time for quiet reflection, and asked themselves what their next best step would be. They determined it would be to focus on growing just two of their most promising ventures while directing their positive energy toward bringing in temporary work that would sustain them until the new ventures flourished.

Within a couple of months they received three highly lucrative contracts (two of which they hadn't even sought out) and had launched their most successful new venture since the inception of their company. Their profits immediately doubled, which they sustained over the eight-month period they last reported. By taking inspired action to terminate the less-than-ideal contract and seek out better options, they opened up possibilities they had never imagined, not only to replace and increase their income, but also to enjoy their work more.

The Right Move. Jodi, a young fund-raising professional, was ready to transition out of a stress-filled job she hated into something healthier and more satisfying for her. She was fearful of leaving the comfort of her current salary and benefits, though, so she started her process by putting herself into a positive energy state—feeling grateful that she had a job at the time that supported her family and provided great benefits, while remaining hopeful about the prospects of finding something that would be an even better fit. She then set her intention to leave her current job within two months, and to be working in a position that afforded her the same type of compensation but a far better mix of work and quality of life. Though she didn't feel "ready" (she was a planner, after all, and thought that she needed to know *exactly* where she was going before taking any job-hunting steps), she decided to get some momentum going by uncharacteristically sending out three résumés on a whim. She was interviewed for all three positions within a two-week period. One requested follow-up information from her, which she promptly sent, but she didn't hear back from them and assumed they had hired someone else, given the pressing time line they stressed to her during the interview.

Prior to practicing inspired action, Jodi's response would have been to say, "Oh well," and give up. In this case, though, she quieted her mind, focused in on her intention, and decided that her next best step would be to contact the company one more time, if only to learn what she could improve upon when she applied next time. She found that the company had never received her follow-up materials, and once they did, they hired her immediately into a position she loves. The job pays well, has far better benefits than her previous job, and provides her with a level of flexibility and creativity she had never imagined. Her inspired action yielded quicker results than she ever thought possible.

Give a Dog a Home. Jim and Teresa, a couple who attended one of my Law of Attraction workshops, had just learned that their beloved dog had run away. They were beside themselves with grief and had looked everywhere and tried everything to find him. They began to think the worst. They decided to put their LOA experiences into practice and opted to choose their state, focusing on appreciation for the time they'd had with the dog and the joy he had brought to them, as well as on optimism that they would find him alive and well. They also detached themselves from the outcome, feeling certain that even if they didn't find their dog, they would be able to handle it.

They set an intention to open themselves up to the variety of ways they might be reunited with their dog. They asked, "What haven't we done and where haven't we looked?" They both thought about the fact that they hadn't gone to the other side of the river near their home, certain that the dog would never find his way over there. They then posted signs in an area across the river that they'd never been to and almost immediately were contacted by the person who had found their dog alive and well. The dog was promptly returned to his joyous owners. They reaped rewards and a slew of dog kisses because they took action, action that didn't necessarily even make sense to them but that they were intuitively moved to take.

An Education in LOA Principles. Kirsten, a midlife communications professional, decided to go back to school to complete her long-desired master's degree. Though she was a bit nervous about how she would manage both the time and the financial commitments of the program, she knew that by choosing her state (one of eager anticipation and joyful energy) and setting her intention (to go back to school with confidence and earn her degree), she would pave the way toward a good educational experience. She didn't know where to start, so she decided to take one inspired action—she called the dean of a local private college to learn more. That one phone call led to the only appointment opening he had in his schedule before leaving town before the start of school. Going to that appointment led to her immediate enrollment as a nonmatriculated student into the ideal program for her. Taking that class led to the program relaxing its admittance requirements so she could enroll as a fully matriculated student for her next class. Taking that next class led to the offer of a graduate assistant role that would pay for her education. That offer made her realize that the assistant position would be too time-consuming, given her professional role and coursework. That, in turn, led to a conversation with her employer, who agreed to increase her work hours slightly to help offset the cost of her tuition. All these wonderful things happened because she took one inspired action—she made one phone call that resulted in a domino effect of steps toward completing her degree. She found it to be quite an education in the LOA in Action!

So now you know the basics about how the LOA *works*. It's time now to look at how you can make it work for *you*. Join me in Part Two for step-by-step instructions for personalizing your practice of the LOA in Action.

PART TWO

HOW TO MAKE
THE LAW
OF ATTRACTION
WORK FOR YOU

Personalizing Your Path

Sowing or Sewing, Working Out or Passing Out

Okay, now it's time for the *action* part of the LOA in Action. While Part One provided an overview of these concepts, Part Two offers you the opportunity to put all the principles and practices into play in your life. Consider it your LOA in Action plan! This part is divided into three chapters, each of which focuses on one of the three steps in the LOA in Action model: Choose Your State, Set Your Intention, and Take Inspired Action. These chapters are followed by a resources section that summarizes a variety of great ways for you to take your learning to the next level.

This part is where you will truly begin to see *results* in your life. Each chapter provides you with an assortment of *action steps* that will propel you forward in your intention. The action step approach is intended as a departure from the idea that changing your life requires you to follow a one-size-fits-all approach. So much of the personal development literature proposes a rigid, prescriptive approach for changing your life . . . a single method that supposedly works for everyone. I believe that rather than looking for a *single* method, we're better off looking for a *simple* method— an à la carte option that allows people to customize their experience in learning, growing, and thriving.

Just as we all have different preferences and personality styles, we all have different approaches to transforming our lives. You understandably have radically different tastes from your colleagues, neighbors, or the person sitting next to you in the coffee shop about what constitutes the perfect home, meal, wardrobe, or morning routine. While one person can't imagine why anyone would want to spend every evening and weekend tending his garden (after all, isn't that what the produce department is for?), another can't conceive of spending every waking hour sewing (because that's why malls exist!). And on a tropical vacation, one person may never dream of missing his daily jog at sunrise (which makes some wonder what he's running *from*), while another feels accomplished having made the leisurely stroll from her room to the pool (after an exhausting attempt to try to find someone to carry her). So whether you're fond of sowing or sewing, working out or passing out, your natural inclinations will always point you in the right direction for you. If we all differ so dramatically in our personal tastes, why wouldn't we embrace different approaches to mastering new skills and using them to enhance our lives? Sounds like common sense to me.

Just as we all have different preferences and personality styles, we all have different approaches to transforming our lives.

Fountain, Flood, Flow

As you move toward mastering the LOA in Action model (Choose Your State, Set Your Intention, and Take Inspired Action), I want to offer one quick thought to help you frame your approach. I like to connect these LOA steps with the images of a flood, a fountain, and the concept of flow.

> *I like to connect these LOA steps with the images of a flood, a fountain, and the concept of flow.*

The *flood* image is about flooding your mind and body with productive thinking and positive energy that keep you in the best state to manifest your dreams. The *fountain* image guides your thinking and insights in ways that spray intention and possibility upward and outward in your life and daily experience. And the *flow* concept goes back to that idea of joyfully (and productively) traveling *with* the current toward your dreams, rather than paddling upstream to get there. When you do that, if you keep your eye on your destination, you can enjoy an exciting and enriching journey toward it, rather than struggling against the natural unfolding of that journey. I encourage you to just keep these images in mind as you move forward to master the action steps in the following chapters.

Time to Act

In years of work with clients and audiences, I have found that there is a tool—or collection of tools—out there to serve nearly every personality type and learning style. Each of the following chapters presents you with an array of these strategies that will help you customize your approach to mastering the LOA. All the action steps are simple and effective, but as with any menu, some options will appeal more to you than others. Sometimes you'll be energetic and ambitious enough to explore several options at once, and sometimes you'll just want to choose something that fills a need for you today (or right now), predictably and efficiently.

Using the action steps, just follow your gut and begin by sampling what sparks your interest based on your unique personality and lifestyle. That will give you a great start to creating lasting change in your life. As I've said before, though, I do encourage you to stretch yourself a bit and be adventurous. Consider giving each method a try *at least once* to see if you might like it or if it produces unexpected benefits for you. Recall that we often identify our favorite new foods or dishes after experimenting a bit and trying something different, and we cultivate new hobbies by dabbling a bit here and there in new pursuits. You might be surprised by what appeals to you after you sample a few options from the action steps. Then, you will have the pleasure of selecting from your old standbys—your favorites—and still have the option of savoring the "new find" when you're in the mood for something that will jazz up your LOA experience just a bit. The nice thing is that all these methods are either centered in science or proven in practice, and they are all as surprisingly simple as they are pleasantly practical. To make completing the exercises easier, I have prepared a free e-workbook that contains full-size copies of the worksheets in this book. Download your copy at www.deannadavis.net. So since our goal here is to put the LOA in Action, let's get busy and *act*.

CHAPTER FIVE

State Shifters:
Action Steps for
Choosing Your State

By now it's no secret that choosing your state is the most important aspect of the LOA in Action model. The success of the other two steps is entirely dependent on your ability to effectively choose your state. As such, this chapter focuses on State Shifters—a variety of simple, straightforward ways to choose your state. These methods help you resonate and harmonize with the very best energy for attracting what you desire in life. When you commit to choosing your state, you program your mind, and thus your intentions and inspired actions, to draw outstanding results to you in *every area of your life*. The more frequently you are in an ideal energy state, the more likely you will be to focus on what you *do* want in life (rather than what you *don't* want), which will dramatically increase your ability to attract the insights and resources you need to morph those desires into reality.

(*When you commit to choosing your state, you program
your mind, and thus your intentions and inspired actions, to
draw outstanding results to you in every area of your life.*)

As the first part of your LOA in Action plan, your action steps for choosing your state are divided into the following areas: GIGO Strategies and Spacemakers. While GIGO strategies focus on the thoughts you consciously put *into* your mind and Spacemakers focus on the thoughts you choose to *release,* they work together synergistically to set the stage for readily attracting your desires. Have fun exploring which methods are most enjoyable—and effective—for you!

Inside Out—GIGO Strategies

As you may recall, our use here of the term *GIGO* differs markedly from its original definition (which was "garbage in, garbage out"). In this case, it means "good in, good out," meaning that if you get into the habit of inserting powerful, positive thoughts *into* your mind, you'll be poised to produce good experiences and results based on what flows *out.* Since an almost infinite number of strategies exist to infuse your brain with goodwill, we'll focus on a couple of techniques that tend to yield the biggest bang for the buck. They include gratitude practices (Thanks! A Lot) and learned optimism (Beyond Pollyanna).

THANKS! A LOT

We usually use the phrase "thanks a lot" in a sarcastic nod toward something undesired. I'm a serious proponent of overhauling both the *meaning* and the *emphasis* in this phrase. I think it should read,

"Thanks! A Lot," because there are few strategies as simple—and as potent—as a daily gratitude practice for enhancing *both* your state *and* your life experience.

> *There are few strategies as simple—and as potent—as a daily gratitude practice for enhancing both your state and your life experience.*

Studies have shown that various gratitude practices can cause both radical spikes in happiness over the short-term *and* significant boosts in happiness over longer periods of time. That's nice in itself, but what's even better is that when we're happier in the *moment*, we're more likely to attract more abundance and success *over time*. Joy and gratitude for the abundance in our lives *now* send a message to our minds, our bodies, and the world around us that *we'd like to experience even more of it in the future, please.*

In the realm of the LOA, gratitude helps create a favorable focus and energy that put you in the ideal state to identify the things you want in your life (or the things you want to avoid) and to open yourself up to receiving them (or avoiding them). Since quantum physics has shown that everything is connected at the energy level, it makes sense that if you place yourself in a positive energy state, you will reap benefits not only physically and emotionally, but also spiritually, relationally, professionally, and financially. The great thing about a daily gratitude practice is that it can be easily mastered and consistently applied with minimal effort and huge rewards. How's that for the total package?

Experts like Dr. Martin Seligman, founder of the Positive Psychology movement, recommend a daily practice of gratitude to create the most favorable mental state conducive to happiness and well-being. What I have found is that people leave one critical element out of their gratitude practices: they tend to turn these practices into the rote (and usually boring) recitation of all the things we shouldn't take for granted. This is about as productive (and as engaging) as reciting your multiplication tables every day. I don't know about you, but I can think of more enjoyable ways to pass the time.

Instead, a truly powerful appreciation process must include the *emotion* behind what you are thankful for. When you focus on the *feeling* that gratitude produces in you, it wells up to the point of overflowing, not only in your emotional state, but also in your life perspective. It's one thing to say, "I'm grateful for my kids," and a completely different thing to clearly *picture* in your mind and *feel* in your body the emotion of profound appreciation for who they are, what they do, and how they impact your life. It's one thing to say, "I appreciate my health," and another to feel sensations throughout your body as you express gratitude for your strong arms, which allow you to lift your precious children in the air, or your great vision, which makes it possible to soak up the glory of an unforgettable sunset. Likewise, it's one thing to say, "I'm fortunate that I have a roof over my head," and another to immerse yourself in appreciation for the warmth during the winter, the comfort of your bed as you sink into it each night, or the exquisite smells coming from the kitchen as you prepare an evening meal.

Often, it's easier to conjure up these powerful emotions when you attach specific images or stories in your mind to the person, item, or experience you're grateful for. One of the most important lessons from neuroscience is that "if you go there in the mind, you can go there in the body." What you're after is what I call the "wave of well-being," that distinct experience of *feeling gratitude wash over you.* It's not just a cognitive *process,* it's a mind/body *celebration.* After all, gratitude is really all about *appreciating* what you have, who you are, and where you are in life right now. One important definition of appreciation is "to increase in value" (as in real estate). So it follows that gratitude practices help you focus on *increasing the value of many things in your life.*

> *A truly powerful appreciation process must include the emotion behind what you are thankful for . . . it's not just a cognitive process, it's a mind/body celebration.*

There are countless ways that you can integrate a daily gratitude practice into your life, and they'll all be equally effective so long as you weave the *feeling* into the *practice.* I've summarized a few options for you here to get you started, but feel free to customize your experience, because ultimately, *it's all about you—* your process and your results. Most of these options can be done in any way that feels appropriate to you—recounting your responses mentally (maybe during your morning routine, your commute, or just before falling asleep), sharing them with someone verbally or in writing (such as a round of gratitude at the dinner table or exchanging emails with a friend on a daily basis) or writing them down (in a journal, on your computer, or on little slips of paper that you keep in a special place). Some processes lend themselves to one method of expression more than another, but you'll find the right fit for you. It doesn't matter *how* you do it, it just matters that you *do it* both *consistently* and *with emotion.* The most important aspect is simply completing the gratitude process on a regular basis in whatever way feels most pleasing to you.

We'll be covering six ways to make gratitude a way of life, including *counting your blessings*, *gratitude journaling*, *gratitude letters*, *wealth walks*, *power showers*, and *abundance practices*. Try some of these ideas on to see how they fit.

Counting Your Blessings. This method involves listing three things that you are grateful for each day and why. Studies have shown that practicing this simple strategy for just two weeks will lead to significantly less depression and more overall happiness for a period of several months. This is one of the practices that Dr. Martin Seligman, author of *Authentic Happiness*, suggests. Imagine how powerful it could be if the process were simply a part of your daily routine all the time. All you do is list three "blessings" you experience each day—three things that went well, that you are grateful for, or that you appreciated about today, and then briefly recount *why* this was important to you. Some people like this process because it's specific, quick, and methodical. It takes only a moment or two but yields a huge return on your investment of time and focus.

Gratitude Journaling. Gratitude journaling is less structured than counting your blessings, in that it involves listing the array of things that you appreciate in your life as they come to mind. It's an ongoing process. You may choose to include people, items, experiences, memories, dreams, or observations—pretty much anything that sparks a moment of thankfulness for you. This process is deceptively simple but exceptionally powerful. It's all a matter of identifying the things in life, big and small (quite honestly it's the small ones we often overlook), that enrich your life. Gratitude journaling has an added bonus of leaving a paper trail, which you can refer to and use to build your resiliency and coping skills during challenging times. If you're not one for written journaling, I'm a huge fan of a resource called the *Gratitude Diet*, which I consider to be a "guided tour of appreciation." It consists of a series of brief daily videos you can watch on your computer, with "gratitude prompts" set to beautiful images, which spark the creative review (and emotional immersion) of everything you appreciate in your life. See "Resources" for more details on this wonderful tool. As brain research tells us, the act of *recalling* the things you appreciate is just as effective in eliciting a positive mind/body response as actually *experiencing* the gratitude firsthand. So even when you're having trouble finding things to be grateful for on a particular day, the process of reviewing previous observations can elevate your spirits and shift your focus toward the possibility of feeling better in the future.

(*Gratitude is all a matter of identifying the things in life, big and small (quite honestly it's the small ones we often overlook), that enrich your life.*)

Gratitude Letter. Researchers have found that the act of writing a "gratitude letter" to someone who has profoundly impacted your life for the better creates a substantial spike in your happiness levels for a full month after sharing the letter with the person in question. Like gratitude journaling, this is one of the favored strategies used by Positive Psychology experts such as Martin Seligman to weave the power of gratitude into your life. Why not take a few moments to pen a heartfelt expression of your thanks and then read it to the person in question? I believe you'll find that this process benefits both you and the recipient, and that it creates a lasting feeling of well-being that encourages you to seek out more people—and more reasons—to be grateful.

Wealth Walk. The Wealth Walk is the simple process of combining a repetitive movement that engages the whole body (walking) with the practice of focused appreciation. All you do is cruise out for a stroll (it can be anywhere from a couple of minutes to a couple of miles), and as you walk, playfully challenge yourself to focus on everything you are grateful for—everything that makes you *wealthy in this moment*. By adding walking to the mix, it enhances your experience in a couple of ways. First, it gives you a rhythm to focus on, and research shows that this kind of repetitive movement can lead to creative breakthroughs, stress reduction, and significantly better health. It's actually a form of active meditation. Second, in the process of walking, you are exposed to different scenery and sensory input (rather than focusing just on the lines in your gratitude journal or the inside of your eyelids!), which literally serve as "prompts" for identifying additional things to be grateful for.

For instance, you might see the flowers in your neighbor's yard and feel gratitude for everything from your eyesight to the beautiful spring day to the power of nature. You might see a child riding a bike and feel appreciation for your own family, for the safety of your neighborhood, or for the array of things like bikes that make our lives more pleasant. Mark my words, you might see a trash can and feel grateful for the fact that you don't have to make a dreaded run to the landfill every week. It's amazing what you can find to be grateful for when you have a rich landscape of examples to choose from (both literally and figuratively). And you'll find through this process that it gets easier and easier to identify the countless things we take for granted on a daily basis that truly contribute to a wonderful way of life for us.

The Power Shower. The Power Shower also uses a mind/body approach to center yourself in thankfulness. It is significant in several ways, first because it is a reminder of those fascinating water studies conducted by Masuro Emoto—recall that emotions and words literally change the structure of water molecules! Second, this method incorporates the sensory input of a shower or bath, which utilizes the power of the mind *and* feedback from the body to anchor you in that potent feeling of appreciation. Third, it's a simple process that dovetails on an already-established habit, which makes it a snap to incorporate as an ongoing practice. It is an outstanding process for reframing your mind and recharging your body with little to no extra effort. Throughout the entire shower or bath, this method asks you to *bathe both your mind and your body* in uplifting energy and emotion. You do this by envisioning everything in your life that is good *right now* and by celebrating the wonderful things and experiences that are *on their way to you* through the LOA in Action.

Abundance Practices. Another fun way to focus on gratitude is to keep notes of appreciation in a special place. Each day, write little reminders of the abundance you experience in your life and drop them into a special basket or box. This is a fabulous alternative for several reasons, including the fact that the basket or box is a *visual reminder* to focus on gratitude. It's also a fun one to incorporate into time with family or friends, with each person taking a turn sharing their note for the day, perhaps around the dinner table. This process makes every day Thanksgiving—no need to wait for an annual holiday to express your appreciation! It's also meaningful to watch the pile of gratitude notes grow and to periodically review them to remind yourself of the wealth of blessings you have in your life, even during times of struggle or strife.

Your *Thanks! A Lot* worksheet summarizes the above-listed gratitude strategies and gives you the opportunity to record your gratitude reflections on a daily basis. Consider selecting at least one gratitude practice to enjoy each day and record your reflections. This will help you determine which techniques feel most *effective* to you, and will catalog your overall *progress* toward mastering the art of appreciation. You can download a free e-workbook of all the LOA in Action worksheets at www.deannadavis.net.

Thanks! A Lot Worksheet

Gratitude practices include (but certainly aren't limited to) the following strategies:

- *Counting your blessings*—List three blessings each day and why you appreciate them.
- *Gratitude journaling*—Keep an ongoing record of what you are thankful for.
- *Gratitude letters*—Write a letter of thanks to someone who has influenced your life.
- *Wealth walks*—Challenge yourself to stay focused on gratitude throughout a walk.
- *Power showers*—Combine active appreciation with the sensory experience of a shower.
- *Abundance baskets*—Write and collect quick reminders of your gratitude triggers.

Select a gratitude practice to implement each day for a week. Record your daily reflections—what you thought about and how it made you feel—and at the end of the week make a few notes about how this process has impacted your life. Commit to mastering the art of appreciation!

Day	Gratitude Practice and Reflections
Monday	
Tuesday	
Wednesday	
Thursday	

(continued from page 130)

Day	Gratitude Practice and Reflections
Friday	
Saturday	
Sunday	
Weekly Reflections	

Gratitude is perhaps one of the easiest—and most potent—strategies for practicing the GIGO method of choosing your state, but there's also another method that research has proven works wonders on both your psyche and your outcomes. That's learned optimism.

BEYOND POLLYANNA

Optimism is a key practice for those who thrive using the LOA in Action, not only because it changes how you *think,* but also because it alters what you *do* (particularly when faced with setbacks or difficulties). According to Positive Psychology, optimism goes far beyond Pollyanna (the fictional character who plays the "glad game" to turn every misfortune into something positive). It is *less* a focus on a "sunny disposition" or "making something good out of every bad," and *more* the mind-set and practices that help people thrive, especially in the presence of challenge or disappointment. Optimism helps determine whether challenges or setbacks cause us to become *motivated to influence our situations* and do what we can to learn and grow, or whether they cause us to *become helpless and hopeless*, thus "shutting down" and failing to use the resources we have to make a difference in our situation now or in the future.

Optimism is a key practice for those who thrive using the LOA in Action, not only because it changes how you think, but also because it alters what you do (particularly when faced with setbacks or difficulties).

The LOA requires that optimism be a part of choosing your state because it is empowering, energizing, and action-oriented. It's a matter of consciously acknowledging the stories we tell ourselves about why things happen and making a decision to distract or dispute *irrational* thinking in favor of cultivating a consistent practice of *productive* thinking. Optimism is one of the most well-researched elements in the field of Positive Psychology, and for good reason. It is both learnable and transformative. When you are disappointed that a date didn't turn out as planned or you didn't get the job you interviewed for, optimism can help reframe the experience in a way that helps you learn more about yourself—and your preferences—so you can both feel better *now* and make better choices in the *future*. So if your date ended up being a complete jerk, optimism helps you pay attention to the characteristics you *do* want to see in a companion, and makes you more likely to attract people in the future who fit that criteria. And if your job interview was a complete disaster, optimism helps you learn from the experience how you can present yourself more effectively next time. In both cases, though, optimism helps ensure that you *won't* become helpless and that you *will* become an active participant in designing your future experiences for the better.

The exercise I recommend using to focus on learned optimism is one that is detailed in my first book, *Living With Intention*. It's called the What/Why/How Method, and it's an excellent— and simple—tool for helping you reorganize your thinking and actions, particularly when faced with disappointments or setbacks. It's a structured means for training yourself to think in ways that support a *productive* state and set the stage for consistent *momentum* toward your intentions. The process does not gloss over the fact that challenging things happen or that they pack an uncomfortable punch. That's just a fact of life. Optimism simply helps you reframe the *situation*—and your *response* to it—in a more rational, constructive way. That, in turn, helps you take action to change what you can to impact your current or future situation. As I described in *Living With Intention*, optimism can feel at times like a "reset" button for your brain and a "restart" button for your action.

> *Optimism can feel at times like a "reset" button for your brain and a "restart" button for your action.*

The strategy is broken down into three steps that ask you to reflect on your situation and respond with constructive action. The first step, *What*, asks you to objectively name the event that happened and pinpoint how it made you feel. The pessimistic style of analyzing an event is typically very *subjective* and highly irrational, while the optimistic style asks you to step back and globally view the situation almost as an observer—with *objectivity*. The second step, *Why*, asks you to identify a variety of factors that could have contributed to this event. Pessimists respond to hardship by looking for all the ways that negative experiences are *their fault*, how the results will be felt for a *long time*, and how they will impact *other areas of their lives*. Optimists, on the other hand, naturally examine the widest range of contributors to the event (since pretty much everything has more than one cause when you really think about it, and usually it's not just because you're the biggest loser of all time or because the world is conspiring against you). Finally, *How* asks you to name how you can influence the situation now or in the future, springboarding you into a state of empowered action. The pessimistic response is simply to shut down, believing that "you can't influence it anyway, so why try?" while the optimistic response is to look for any point of leverage in the way you think, feel, or act to make a difference in the situation now or in the future.

To expand your GIGO options, give yourself the gift of optimism by mastering this easy technique and using it often. The *Beyond Pollyanna* worksheet takes you through the process in a quick and effective way.

Beyond Pollyanna Example

The following is an example of the Beyond Pollyanna process:

Challenge or hardship I'm facing: I am so upset. I recently went back to school to get my degree—a goal I've had for many years. I was so excited and I love my classes. I feel like I'm really "in my element" in school. All of a sudden, though, my kids are acting out and complaining that I'm never around. I'm feeling guilty half of the time and frustrated with them the other half of the time, even though I want to really be enjoying this experience at school and I want to feel like a good mom. This feels like it's taking all of the joy out of this experience I've waited so long for.

What (what has objectively happened and how do I feel?): Well, objectively, I simply went back to school (and I'm loving it). I guess that also means that it changed the way we schedule our time around the house and for activities. And it means that I'm spending some time on school that I used to spend with the kids (or doing things for the kids). On one hand, I feel incredible—school is a dream come true for me. On the other hand, I feel guilty about taking time away from the kids to spend on myself, and I also feel frustrated (and honestly . . . sometimes resentful) because they are old enough to understand that Mom needs to have a life, too, but they're still complaining.

Why (list an assortment of reasons why this could have happened): I guess the kids are just not used to me devoting some of my time to myself. I've always been available to them 24/7—that's what they're used to, so I'm sure it feels weird to them. The fact is, though, that I still spend tons of quality time with them—and quantity time, for that matter, too. I suppose I could have contributed to this dynamic a bit because I didn't really think to help them transition into this new routine. Even though I know they're happy for me, it's a change from what they're used to. It also just so happens that my schooling started at the beginning of their school year—a big time of change for them. That might have made it more difficult for them, since they were dealing with their own changes and mine.

How (what are some ways that I can influence this situation?): First, I'm going to sit down and talk with them about my school, to let them know I've noticed they seem frustrated. I'm going to share with them how important it is to me and how much joy it brings me. Then, I'm going to ask for their input on how we can all be happy with the new schedule. Maybe we can brainstorm ideas so that the time we

(continued from page 135)

spend together is focused on what they say is most important to them instead of what I think is most important to them. And maybe we can come up with ways to spend time together that incorporate my school . . . like maybe we can all do our homework together? Ultimately, I want this to be an opportunity to teach them that, as a family, we can always work through changes in a respectful way together. In the future, when I make a major life change like this, I'm going to try to spend a bit more time helping them be a part of making the transition successful from the start. And when possible, I'll do my best to help spread out transitions over time so the kids aren't experiencing too many things at once. Finally, I'm going to continue focusing on how much I enjoy school and how important it is to me, because as I do that, I will not only be pursuing my own dream, but also be a great role model for my kids to learn how they can pursue theirs.

There are other books that offer step-by-step guidance for integrating optimism into your life, including Martin Seligman's *Learned Optimism* and *Authentic Happiness*. See "Resources" for these and other great books.

While gratitude and optimism strategies help you purposefully choose what you put *into* your mind, it's equally important to focus on what you *release* from it. That's why Spacemaker strategies are so important—they purge from your mind what you *don't* want in there in order to make more room for what you *do* want.

Spacemakers

I just have to come right out and say it. In general, it's the "negative mojo factor" that tends to keep people circling the drain, on the brink of spending untold amounts of their lives swirling around in

Beyond Pollyanna Worksheet

Review this brief summary of how to use the What/Why/How Method, and then apply this strategy to an example in your own life.

1. **What.** First, identify the *what*, or the challenge you are facing that could cause you to shut down or get into a space of negativity or victimization. Be very clear about what *objectively* has happened, and then name how it made you feel, whether you are disappointed, disillusioned, frustrated, fearful, or experiencing any number of other uncomfortable emotions.
2. **Why.** Then, identify an assortment of *whys* associated with your current situation. Your goal is to name the variety of things that may have contributed to the mishap. Remember, there are usually a variety of things that can influence a single outcome.
3. **How.** Finally, select a *how* or two that will help you influence the situation. Ask yourself, "How will I change my attitude, environment, or actions to make a difference in this situation now or in the future?" Your answer may include one or all of these elements to help you effectively navigate your current struggle.

Challenge or hardship I'm facing:

What (what has objectively happened and how do I feel?):

Why (list an assortment of reasons why this could have happened):

How (what are some ways that I can influence this situation?):

the sewer of discontent. Perhaps a nicer way of saying this is that one of the most significant reasons people keep themselves "stuck" in a trajectory toward everything unfulfilling in life is that they begin defining themselves and their experiences through negativity, irrational thinking, limiting beliefs, or other unproductive ways of thinking. It's not to say that challenging things *don't* happen or that we should *ignore* them when they do. It's not to say that we should be able to let every misfortune roll off us like water off a duck's back. And it's not to say that our main mission in life should be to avoid all negative feelings like the plague.

On the contrary, Positive Psychology would say that you absolutely *must* acknowledge challenges and setbacks, learn what you need to from them, and then decide how you want to influence your situation and/or your future (just as you learned in "Beyond Pollyanna"). The problem is, sometimes people get so caught up in the emotional turmoil of it all that they find themselves unlikely— or at times unable—to move from emotional incapacitation to engage their rational mind to do something constructive. That's where releasing techniques, or *Spacemakers*, come into play. There are a variety of methods, but the good ones all have in common the capacity to help you *gently distance yourself from the emotional "charge" of a situation long enough to make conscious decisions about how you want to feel or what you want to do about it.*

> *Spacemakers (releasing strategies) have the capacity to help you gently distance yourself from the emotional "charge" of a situation long enough to make conscious decisions about how you want to feel or what you want to do about it.*

The whole idea behind Spacemakers is the concept of releasing—you are, in effect, "clearing out" space in your mind and body to make room for new beliefs, visions, and habits that support your life goals. I call this whole shebang "release and replace." It's sort of like the idea of cleaning out your closets. You get rid of all the clothes you hate, that don't fit you anymore, or that went out of style during the Great Depression (or during your own personal great depression) so that you can make room for a new wardrobe that suits your style, body, and century. Our old emotional hang-ups and fixations tend to be like those old clothes that don't really serve a purpose except to take up space that could be occupied by something far more useful (and fashionable, for that matter).

So if you have negative associations about making money (it's hard to do, there's no way to sustain it, I always lose it), it's time to release them. Or if you have limiting beliefs about finding your soul mate (all the good ones are taken, no one is committed anymore, no one would want me anyway), it's time to let go of them. And if you have self-sabotaging ways of thinking about your health (I've always been fat and always will be, I just have to live with the misery of this chronic condition, it's too hard to change my bad habits), it's time to create space for something new that serves you.

The most important part of releasing is to find a method or two that work for *you* and then to use them on a regular basis to achieve a favorable state that attracts more of what you want (and less of what you don't want) into your life. Try using some of these methods on simple stressors throughout the day, and then on low-key habitual ways of thinking or challenging events. Build your Spacemaker muscles by practicing *first* on minor irritations, such as an interaction with a rude store clerk or a pet peeve at the weekly staff meeting, and then graduate to using the strategies to release more significant challenges, such as self-esteem issues, relationship struggles, or long-term negative habits. Spacemaker practices include meditation (Peace of Mind), Emotional Freedom Technique (A Different Kind of Buzz), and the Sedona Method (The Invitation).

PEACE OF MIND

Meditation is one of those words that tends to scare people off, conjuring up images of yogis on mountaintops chanting obscure mantras or religious fanatics chasing people through airports. For some reason, my clients and audiences always seem to have the idea that meditation is hopelessly mysterious and painfully difficult to master. None of these assessments could be farther from the truth. My personal interpretation of meditation is that you *simply find a process of introducing silence and stability to replace the frenetic activity of your mind.* By doing this, you effectively reduce the stress response in the body and the incessant chatter in the brain long enough to experience relaxation, peace, creativity, and focus—states favorable to putting the LOA in Action. Through meditation, you also have the opportunity to release fear, judgment, and limiting beliefs that can keep you from choosing a productive state or setting a powerful intention.

Researchers have found that the regular practice of meditation has a positive impact on everything from your physical health (less pain, faster healing, lower blood pressure, heightened immune function, etc.) to your emotional health (less stress, lower rates of depression, reduced anxiety, etc.). It is associated with increased activity in the part of the brain associated with happiness and positive thoughts and emotions. It has also been found to be an outstanding tool for enhancing focus, memory, learning, creative insights, problem solving, and heightened awareness. Oh, and there's so much more.

Studies now show that meditation coordinates and synchronizes the left and right sides of the brain (which are usually out of sync), and actually has the same impact on the mind—through training and actual physical modification—as sports or athletic conditioning has on the body. Researchers have shown that the brain is continually developing throughout life, and that practices such as meditation can actually *rewire* the brain—a characteristic they refer to as neuroplasticity. Dr. Richard Davidson, a neuroscientist at the University of Wisconsin, notes that for long-term meditation practitioners, "Their mental practice is having an effect on the brain in the same way golf or tennis practice will enhance performance."

> *The brain is continually developing throughout life, and practices such as meditation can actually* rewire *the brain.*

While there are many types of meditation practices, there are two categories of meditation that tend to help clarify the different approaches. They are *concentrative meditation* and *mindfulness meditation.*

Concentrative Meditation. In concentrative meditation, your intent is to focus on something such as your breath, a word or phrase (mantra), counting, an item/image (like a candle), a concept (such as compassion), or some other form of concentration. The purpose is to gently release all other thoughts (not to fight against them or force them out, just simply to acknowledge them, allow them to go, and gently redirect your attention to the object of focus). This type of meditation has been studied in many ways, showing outstanding benefits for body, mind, and spirit.

I find the most beneficial effects to be when you make meditation easy, accessible, and pleasant, including creating a sacred space that feels comforting to you, using tools that help you transition into meditation (candles, music, aromatherapy, mats, or pillows). If "sitting" meditation isn't your thing, other practices might interest you more. Why not try yoga or tai chi, use guided meditation or brain-sync audio CDs, or engage in a focused, repetitive activity such as walking or knitting/crocheting, perhaps while counting rhythmically? There is no right or wrong way to meditate—the idea is to simply allow the brain to quiet itself enough to *release thought* and bask in gentle, *focused silence*. My favorite resources for focused meditation include those by Herbert Benson (*The Relaxation Response* and *The Breakout Principle*). See "Resources" for other great books and audios.

$$\Big(\quad \begin{array}{c} \textit{There is no right or wrong way to meditate—the idea is to} \\ \textit{simply allow the brain to quiet itself enough to } \text{release} \\ \text{thought } \textit{and bask in gentle, } \text{focused silence.} \end{array} \quad \Big)$$

Mindfulness Meditation. Mindfulness meditation allows you to act as an impartial observer, experiencing every aspect of the present moment. Jon Kabat-Zinn, one of the most respected researchers and teachers of this methodology, refers to it as "moment-to-moment nonjudgmental awareness." It typically includes focusing on the breath, but more as a tool to enhance relaxation, while bringing your attention to the present moment and your awareness to your current experience. Rather than *directing* your focus or thought, you are simply *paying attention*—fully aware of what you are experiencing in the here and now. Your role is *not* to judge or to try to change your focus from what you observe; it's more a matter of simply drinking in your experience in this moment, whether you are washing your hands or watching the sunset, walking up the stairs or waking up in the morning. The key is simply to attend to all aspects of your experience—your senses, surroundings, movements, and thoughts—and immerse yourself in the present moment. I particularly like Jon Kabat-Zinn's books (for example, *Wherever You Go, There You Are*) and audios (such as *Mindfulness Meditation for Beginners*) for learning to practice mindfulness. See "Resources" for additional ideas.

> *Your role is not to judge or to try to change your focus from what you observe; it's more a matter of simply drinking in your experience in this moment.*

Explore and Experience Meditation. I strongly recommend learning more about which style of meditation you prefer, and that you go through a process of customizing a meditation approach that works for you. There is no right or wrong approach—it's just a matter of finding a practice that feels good to you and that serves as a Spacemaker in your mind and your life. For the purpose of practice, I'll describe here a very simple process of focusing on your breath that can be a wonderful starting point for cultivating a personal meditation practice.

Sit in a comfortable position and focus on your breathing. Pay attention to the rhythmic movement of the air in and out of your nostrils, how it fills your lungs and slowly exits the body. If it helps to focus on the sensation of your diaphragm rising and falling or the imagery of the air flowing into your lungs, feel free to do that.

Some people find it helpful to count to four or eight as they inhale and exhale to offer gentle guidance to the mind. Still others appreciate the sound of a ticking clock or a metronome to stay focused on their breath. Whatever works for you is fine, as long as you are relaxing the body and allowing the mind to release its flood of frenetic thoughts and come to a resting state—a quiet, peaceful state.

Inevitably, thoughts will continue to make themselves known in your mind. In those instances your only role is to *notice* them (not to analyze or judge them) and to allow them to dissipate as you return your focus to your breath. Some people make the mistake of trying to force those thoughts out, which ends up being counterproductive and actually draws *more* thoughts and more activity into your mind. You are not the thought police here; you are just an observer who gently and consistently redirects your focus to your breathing.

You are not the thought police here; you are just an observer who gently and consistently redirects your focus to your breathing.

Give yourself the opportunity to practice this meditation several times a day, starting with just a few minutes and working your way up to ten or twenty (depending on your preference). Sometimes a couple of minutes are enough to clear your thoughts and refresh your focus, and other times a longer period gives you the "sustained release" effect of peace and space in the mind. Just take a relaxed, playful approach with the process and see what works for you. There is no right or wrong way to do it.

As you practice this technique, it's helpful to record some of your observations about what the experience feels like, and what it yields for you. You can do this using the following *Peace of Mind* worksheet.

Peace of Mind Worksheet

Review these quick reminders about the meditative process:

- Sit in a comfortable position.
- Focus on your breathing.
- If desired, focus on sensations or visualization (air filling your lungs), rely on counting, or rely on a ticking clock or a metronome to gently guide your focus to your breathing.
- When thoughts present themselves, simply observe them and allow them to float away while you return your focus to your breathing.

Record a week's worth of your observations and reflections about your meditation experience here:

Monday

Tuesday

Wednesday

Thursday

Friday

(continued from page 145)

Saturday

Sunday

Sure, silence is golden but sometimes it's just not enough. Meditation only goes so far as a Spacemaker, particularly if you have a significantly negative emotion you are struggling with or pervasive thoughts that you are having trouble releasing. In those cases, focused attention and targeted strategies can help release those unpleasant thoughts that might be holding you back. That's where the next few strategies come into play.

A DIFFERENT KIND OF BUZZ

I first learned about Emotional Freedom Technique (EFT) from a friend and colleague, Ingrid Agnew, who is a gifted practitioner of this practice. A peak performance specialist, Ingrid helps everyone from athletes to business owners "improve their mental game" by releasing emotional blocks and ingrained patterns of negative thinking, among other things. The first time my husband practiced it, it immediately improved his golf game (sadly, it didn't improve his rather unorthodox stance). And the first time I tried it, I felt one of the most profound—and immediate—releases of negative emotion I have ever experienced in my life. Thousands of examples show the positive impact of the EFT methodology on everything from depression to weight loss and on physical pain to financial abundance. It has been used to address trauma (even with war veterans and crime victims), assist people in quitting smoking, and decrease test anxiety. It's also used to reduce the power that limiting beliefs or unproductive habits can have in keeping you from experiencing success in various areas of your life. And that's just a small list of the applications. As such, I am a huge fan of EFT as a tool for neutralizing the "buzz" around negative or unproductive emotions.

In my interpretation and practice, EFT is a self-applied form of acupuncture (actually acupressure, since thankfully there are no needles involved). It uses simple "tapping" techniques, combined with a series of verbal statements, to help release the unpleasant thought pattern or feeling. I always imagine it as lessening the "charge" of a difficult emotion and resetting the connection between my mind and body so it won't create a vicious cycle of negative thinking, followed by a physical stress response, which then perpetuates the negative thinking. I see EFT as a tool for creating a type of "pattern interrupt" that gets me out of my negative thinking death spiral and into a state of relative peace and calm (or at least less discomfort). It's that calmer state that supports creative problem-solving and objective assessments, or makes unproductive, knee-jerk responses less likely.

The "shortcut version" of EFT simply involves tapping certain points on your hand, face, torso, wrists, and head while saying a specific phrase that focuses on the emotion you want to release or neutralize. There are also more lengthy versions of the method that can be used on more challenging issues (such as phobias, traumas, or long-standing negative emotional patterns). In either case, you can learn the method through a trained provider in your area, or through books and video programs that demonstrate the strategy and how to use it. Perhaps my favorite aspect of EFT, though, is that once you learn it, you are able to self-administer it any time.

It is beyond the scope of this book—and beyond my personal expertise—to teach you the EFT methodology here, but I cannot recommend this technique highly enough. I have seen lives completely transformed through the application of this simple process. "Resources" provides an overview of the very best resources I have found to learn EFT and apply it in your life. I strongly encourage you to take your learning—and mastery—of this powerful practice to the next level. *The Buzz and the Invitation* worksheet provides space for you to learn and reflect on your application of EFT (and the Sedona Method, discussed below) in your life.

THE INVITATION

Another technique that I personally practice and that my clients have found to be instrumental in helping them release negative emotions or unproductive ways of thinking is called the Sedona Method. The strategy is described in Hale Dwoskin's *New York Times* bestselling book of the same name, as well as in a variety of audio and video programs and transformative in-person seminars. My personal view on the Sedona Method is that it is a way of consciously putting more "space" in between your negative thoughts, giving you respite from the reinforcing cycle of negative thinking, so that eventually the space becomes bigger than the negative thought. It is powerful in its simplicity (almost deceptively so), in that one of its most common practices only requires that you ask yourself a series of questions about your "readiness" to let go of a negative or unproductive thought. That's all it is—offering yourself an "invitation" to let go of a painful emotion rather than holding on to it so tightly and thinking you must do so forever. There are no right or wrong ways of responding to the questions, but each time you ask them, you are in a way inviting yourself to respond affirmatively to the question of when you will be ready to release the unpleasant thought. Eventually this process usually leads to making the decision to go ahead and release it.

> *That's all it is—offering yourself an "invitation" to let go of a painful emotion rather than holding on to it so tightly and thinking you must do so forever.*

I had the pleasure of watching Hale Dwoskin give an enlightening presentation on the method. I was particularly struck by the example he shared of how we tend to get used to holding on to things and forget that it's always in our power to let go of them if we choose. He asked us to hold up a pen and grasp it as tightly as possible in our fist. He asked the audience to identify how it felt, which garnered responses like "uncomfortable," "hard," and "unpleasant." He then asked everyone to open his or her hand and allow the pen to gently roll around in the palm, and again asked for opinions about how this felt. Responses included "relaxed," "better," and "relief." Then, he instructed the audience members to turn their hands over and allow the pen to gently drop to the ground, again asking them what this experience felt like. People chimed in with words like "empowering" and "easy."

The lesson I took away was that we have as many options regarding our thoughts and emotions as we do with that pen—we can grasp them tightly and learn to bear the discomfort and unpleasantness, eventually identifying ourselves with the ongoing pain associated with them, or we can choose to open up and allow those difficult thoughts and emotions to roll around for a while, observing them, deciding if we want to learn from or use them constructively in some way and, if not, we can simply choose to drop them. What a concept!

I love the fact that the Sedona Method can be done at any time, anywhere without anyone knowing that you are even using the technique. It is entirely a matter of *silently* asking yourself questions and giving yourself the space and time to *decide* how you want to respond to them. So many people allow their thinking—particularly their negative thinking—to perpetually idle on autopilot, rather than taking the controls and determining the direction they want to go with those thoughts. Doesn't the latter sound much more productive?

As with EFT, it is beyond the scope of this book to offer an in-depth training on the Sedona Method. It is best learned by reading the book, listening to audios or watching videos, or attending an in-person training event. I cannot stress enough how effective this strategy is as a Spacemaker. If you are serious about releasing resistance and allowing yourself to attract the experiences you really want to attract into your life, I highly recommend learning and regularly practicing the Sedona Method. "Resources" lists a book and a website that will help you move toward mastery of this exceptional tool. *The Buzz and the Invitation* worksheet provides space for you to learn and reflect on your application of the Sedona Method (and the previously mentioned EFT) in your life.

Now that you have learned and practiced an assortment of strategies for effectively choosing your state, you are ready to move into learning more about the kind of life you want to live and how you can get from here to there. Chapter Six focuses on just that—visiting Intention Central to master action steps for setting your intention.

The Buzz and the Invitation Worksheet

Emotional Freedom Technique (EFT) and the *Sedona Method* are two phenomenal Spacemaker resources. They help you learn to release negative thought patterns and unproductive emotions that could be inhibiting your ability to put the LOA in Action. They are powerful processes that are best learned from their original sources and practiced on a regular basis. Review the basic concepts for each method and then seek out your preferred resources for putting these outstanding strategies into practice in your life.

1. *EFT*—a form of self-applied acupuncture/acupressure, combined with phrases that help you decrease the "buzz" in the mind and body associated with negative thoughts or unproductive emotions. Resources include free workbooks and an online newsletter (as well as comprehensive audio, video, and training programs), found online at www.emofree.com. Also look for certified practitioners in your area to attend local workshops and/or receive one-on-one consulting to help you personalize the technique.

   Notes on what you learned about *EFT* and how you plan to apply it in your life:

2. *The Sedona Method*—a cognitive process involving asking yourself a series of brief questions that create "space" in between negative thoughts or unproductive emotions and invite you to release your hold on these feelings. Resources include the *New York Times* bestselling book *The Sedona Method* and a variety of free introductory resources (as well as excellent audio, video, and training programs), found online at www.sedonamethod.com.

   Notes on what you learned about the *Sedona Method* and how you plan to apply it in your life:

CHAPTER SIX

Intention Central:
Action Steps for
Setting Your Intention

As you've already learned, setting your intention involves a few key steps. First, you assess where you are *now* to set the stage for where you want to *be*. These strategies are described in the section "You Are Here." Second, you sift through your *preferences* and *possibilities* so that you have an idea of the range of options you have for living the life you desire. These techniques are covered in "Sifting Strategies." And finally, you make a *decision*—you create an intention with certainty and conviction—about the life you want to lead. You will find these practices in "The Deciding Factor." Enjoy the process of exploring your options and setting your intentions!

You Are Here

One step that will help you personalize your path toward putting the LOA in Action is to identify your "here." Whether you're in a mall, at the airport, or at a highway rest stop, you'll always find maps showing you the lay of the land. Inevitably, there's always a red dot or flag somewhere that shouts, "YOU ARE HERE," which gives you perspective—a global picture of where you stand in the grand scheme of things. From that flag, you know your options for navigating from where you are now to where you want to be. So before we go any further, let's take a moment to identify two things: where your "here" *is* and exactly what it *looks* like and *feels* like. It's a simple matter of assessing your current life situation and outcomes so you have a clear picture of where you're traveling *from* and why you want to journey from where you are *now* to where you want to *go*.

As you move toward setting your intention, this first step is all about assessing how things are in your life right now. You will identify both what is working *well*, so you can retain and build on these strengths, as well as the *contrast* that exists—the factors in your life that aren't as you would like them to be right now—so that you can craft a vision for how you would like to transform these areas of your life. Looking at this contrast is actually a good thing, because the only way we know *bad* is because we can compare it to *good*; *right* has more meaning when we know its converse—*wrong*; and we can clearly identify *light* because we know its opposite—*dark*. The same holds true in our lives. If we can identify the contrast—what *isn't* exactly what we'd like it to be right now—we can then focus our primary attention on its opposite—what we'd *prefer* to be experiencing—to gain vivid clarity about our preferences, possibilities, and intentions.

What's most important here, though, is that too many people get caught up in focusing on the contrast. They fixate on their disappointment or disillusionment in the here and now so much that they don't effectively envision how things could be different in the future, whether that future is two minutes, two months, or two years from now. They get a sort of "tunnel vision" that keeps them expecting that more of the same is headed their way, instead of focusing their attention and energy on the opportunities that exist for change. So, the rule of thumb here is to *spend only a short period of time identifying the contrast in your life,* and then to *move immediately* into the exercises that help you craft a vision—and an intention—for how you want things to be different. The process is more about setting the stage for you to focus on your *desire* rather than lamenting about what you *lack.*

(*The process is more about setting the stage for you to focus on your* desire *rather than lamenting about what you* lack.)

Take a few moments to complete your *You Are Here* worksheet. This process will help you identify exactly where you are now in seven key areas of your life, and precisely what that "here" looks like for you. The seven life areas are: Health and Well-Being (Body/Mind/Spirit); Financial Well-Being; Professional Success and Fulfillment; Relationships; Fun and Recreation; Lifestyle; and Contribution and Legacy. Begin by circling the number associated with how satisfied you are in each area of your life, and then make a few notes for each area that detail what's working *well* and which outcomes are *not* what you would like them to be at this time. Then jot down a few reflections about what you learned through this process and what opportunities you have in each area of your life. Your role is to be an *objective* analyst here—just survey your current experiences, feelings, and outcomes in each area of your life, and like a scientist, make notes about what you find *interesting.* Avoid judging or complaining, and instead, simply focus on *observing.*

Once you have completed your *You Are Here* worksheet, it's time to identify one of the seven areas of your life that you'd like to focus on for the remaining exercises in this section. This is just for the sake of allowing you to explore the remaining strategies in a particular area of your life, to avoid getting overwhelmed or distracted by too many options. You are welcome—in fact, encouraged!—to complete these exercises for each and every area of your life, but for the sake of mastering the processes and creating meaningful change in your life right now, it's helpful to focus in on one key area. This exercise is decidedly *not* a reflection of your *values*—it *isn't* about which life areas you think are most important to you overall. This worksheet is meant to help you identify which areas you want to devote significant effort to improve *right now*. So if you rate financial well-being or professional success and fulfillment higher than relationships and health, it does not mean that you think these things are more important; it simply means that these are the areas you are most drawn to work on at this point in your life! With that in mind, complete your *Life Area Hierarchy* worksheet.

Sifting Strategies

Once you know where you are *now*, you can start the process of identifying where you'd like to *go*. The following strategies invite you to sift through your preferences and possibilities so that you can then set your intention for transforming each area of your life. All these techniques are simply designed to help you begin *paying attention* to your desires. They help you piece together a picture of the things you miss out on when you live your life on autopilot—all the things you take for granted, the dreams you once had, the

You Are Here Worksheet

Part I: Assess Your Satisfaction

	Completely Dissatisfied	Dissatisfied	A Little Dissatisfied	Neutral	A Little Satisfied	Satisfied	Completely Satisfied
Health and Well-Being (Body/Mind/Spirit)	1	2	3	4	5	6	7
Financial Well-Being	1	2	3	4	5	6	7
Professional Success and Fulfillment	1	2	3	4	5	6	7
Relationships	1	2	3	4	5	6	7
Fun and Recreation	1	2	3	4	5	6	7
Lifestyle	1	2	3	4	5	6	7
Contribution and Legacy	1	2	3	4	5	6	7

(continued from page 157)

Part II: What's Working, What's Not

	What's Working	What's Not Working
Health and Well-Being (Body/Mind/Spirit)		
Financial Well-Being		
Professional Success and Fulfillment		
Relationships		
Fun and Recreation		
Lifestyle		
Contribution and Legacy		

Part III: Reflections and Opportunities

	Reflections and Opportunities for Change
Health and Well-Being (Body/Mind/Spirit)	
Financial Well-Being	
Professional Success and Fulfillment	
Relationships	
Fun and Recreation	
Lifestyle	
Contribution and Legacy	

Life Area Hierarchy Worksheet

Spend a moment in silent reflection about the following seven areas of your life. Think about what you are *currently* experiencing and what you *desire* to be experiencing in each of these areas. Then, prioritize them in order of which areas are most important for you to focus your attention and energy on first. Just go with your gut instinct and rank them from 1 to 7, with 1 being your *highest* priority for life change right now and 7 being your *lowest* priority. Then note at the bottom of the worksheet what your priority area is.

Important note: This exercise is not meant to be a reflection of your *values*—it isn't about which areas you think are most important to you overall. The worksheet is meant to help you identify which areas you want to devote significant effort to improve *right now*. So if you rate financial well-being or professional success and fulfillment higher than relationships and health, it does not mean that you think these things are more important; it simply means that these are the areas you are most drawn to work on at this point in your life!

- [ ] Health and Well-Being (Body/Mind/Spirit)

- [ ] Financial Well-Being

- [ ] Professional Success and Fulfillment

- [ ] Relationships

- [ ] Recreation and Fun

- [ ] Lifestyle

- [ ] Contribution and Legacy

My top priority area for life change right now:

little insights that give you that twinge of excitement. They encourage you to say "what if?" and "why not?" rather than "oh well" and "not again." They help you become consistently mindful of the rich tapestry of opportunity that exists in your life.

(*These techniques are simply designed to help you begin paying attention to your desires . . . They help you become consistently mindful of the rich tapestry of opportunity that exists in your life.*)

Your sifting strategies are broken down into three exercises: *I Desire*, *Shopping Cart*, and *Mind Movie*. Have fun with these processes—they can be as engaging (and even entertaining) as they are enlightening. It's revealing if you complete one of them, and can be stunningly intriguing when you complete all three. You make the choice—customize your experience as you wish!

I DESIRE

I love this exercise, which I originally experienced at one of Jack Canfield's workshops. It's one that I personally repeat on a regular basis because I find that it reveals everything from subtle changes to huge epiphanies in what I desire out of life, and everything in between. It's a straightforward yet exceptionally powerful process that helps tap into some of the below-the-surface preferences that you're not necessarily conscious of all the time. The process is best done with a partner so that you can do some free-flowing brainstorming *and* so that you're less likely to edit your responses as you go along (because your partner is recording them for you). It can also be effective if you do it alone as a journaling exercise or even if you speak your responses into a voice recorder. I'll describe it here as a partner exercise but I encourage you to move forward with it in the way that feels best to you.

Begin by giving your *I Desire* worksheet to your partner. Your partner's role is twofold: (1) to ask you repeatedly, "What do you desire?" and (2) to record your answers for you. The pace should be relaxed but consistent, and your only role is to share the first thing that comes to mind each time he or she asks the question. Your goal is *not* to filter, judge, or edit your responses, it is to simply *respond*. Spend at least a good ten minutes on this exercise (feel free to set a timer so you can allow your mind to wander without having to watch the clock) . . . long enough to feel as if you have fully explored all the things in your life that you desire right now, from immediate interests to quirky ideas, and from short-term items to long-term goals. Be sure to include an array of lifetime dreams and values. Nothing is off-limits and everything is fair game.

If you allow yourself to truly relax into this process, you might be amazed at the items that wind up on your list. Things you used to love but had forgotten about, dreams you once had but put on the back burner, desires that would make your day-to-day life more pleasant but you have forgotten to focus on. For example, your list might include everything from waking up to your favorite coffee to falling asleep during a deep-tissue massage or pinching yourself as your long-held dream of selling your art comes true. It could include something as simple as your fondness for rock climbing or something as lofty as your desire to climb the ranks of public office. Or it could include a goal to mend fences with a relative or mend the pile of clothing at the back of your closet. Your list—and your desires—are uniquely yours.

Once you finish your list, your next step is to go through and

I Desire Worksheet

I desire . . .

circle the ones that jump out at you as surprising or intriguing or notable. There's no ranking that needs to take place here . . . it's all just a process of examining what you found and looking for the things that spark the greatest interest and/or insight. These are the things that you can muse on for a while to see what intentions might emerge from these desires and preferences.

SHOPPING CART

The *Shopping Cart* exercise can be used as an alternative—or better yet, an addition—to the *I Desire* exercise, as it is a highly visual and an ongoing method of collecting ideas about how you would like your life to be. It's also an outstanding way to begin preparing to create your vision board(s), which we'll cover later. For this process, you begin by collecting ideas and reminders of what you would like to experience, feel, have, do, or be in your life and keep them together in a convenient container for easy access.

The reminders can be pictures from catalogs, magazines, or online sources; they can be postcards or photographs, stories, quotes, or phrases. You could include Post-it notes to remind yourself of something you saw or thought of, journal pages that explore specific desires in-depth, or even tangible objects that represent key desires (such as a seashell or a swatch of fabric).

Your container can be anything—a simple shoebox, a three-ring binder or spiral-bound notebook, a file folder, or a drawer. It could be something as mundane as an office-supply in-box or as elaborate as a hand-carved treasure chest. Whether you want to focus on function or form or both, just find something that keeps all your preferences and desires close at hand so that you can add to the mix and review your collection at any time. The idea is simply to go through a process of broadening your perspective to survey the rich array of preferences that might enhance your life, and then to collect those insights in some way to allow your mind the luxury of processing it all over time. With ongoing practices like this, you will be better poised to identify specific intentions you would like to set in your life.

While many people focus on the tangible things they would like to acquire in their life (and there's nothing wrong with this), such as homes, cars, gadgets, and gizmos, I'll ask you to stretch yourself a bit further than this to capture not only what you want to *have* but also how you want to *feel* and who you want to *be*. So you certainly may include that new car, but it's as important to focus on who is sitting in it with you, where you are traveling to, and what kind of freedom (or joy or adventure) it brings you. And certainly you *will* want to include that dream home, but what will it yield for you—family time, solitude, or a place to savor your favorite pastimes? The point is to create the most vivid picture of the life you want to design using this method, and then to review it often. Remember, by frequently focusing on what you *desire*, you train the brain to place those things into its "important" file, which makes you more likely to recognize the *opportunities* and *resources* that will help you attain them. The *Shopping Cart* worksheet will help you set the stage for a productive shopping experience!

Remember, by frequently focusing on what you desire, you train the brain to place those things into its "important" file, which makes you more likely to recognize the opportunities and resources that will help you attain them.

Shopping Cart Worksheet

1. Identify the life area you will be focusing on:

2. Indentify the container you will be using to collect your shopping cart images:

3. Where will you keep it?

4. Now, begin collecting all those images and reminders and placing them in your receptacle. *Begin today* and *review your shopping cart regularly* to remind yourself of all those wonderful preferences that you can translate into intentions!

MIND MOVIE

The *Mind Movie* process is a method of getting to a level of vivid imagination and visualization about *exactly* how you want a particular aspect of your life to unfold. In this exercise, you are the writer, director, choreographer, and star of your future life story. The process asks that you set aside some quiet time in a relaxing space to dream about how you want that element of your life to *look*, *feel*, and *be*. Close your eyes and picture yourself living your dreams, using every sensory detail you can. You are an *active participant* in this mind movie, *not* an observer. What do you see, smell, touch, taste, and hear? Who is with you, what is happening, and how do you feel? Color in every aspect of the picture that you can. Play with camera angles and have fun with close-ups and panoramas. Get as artsy as you wish. Add music and sound effects, or turn the pace of activity up or down. Use subtitles and credits if you wish.

For instance, if you are imagining your physical well-being, it's not just a matter of how you look, but how are you moving, what are you doing, what are you wearing, and what scenery is around you? What are you eating and drinking, how do your muscles feel, how do you view yourself? What is noticeably present—or absent? What are you thinking and what are you saying? Get to an exquisite level of detail *until you feel that you are already there*, basking in this amazing experience. The example on the next page illustrates how one person used the *Mind Movie* process to explore one area of her life. But don't let this example limit you . . . let your imagination be your guide. You can create anything you want in this exercise, so grab your *Mind Movie* worksheet and record everything you can about your Oscar-worthy outcome!

Not Just Window Shopping

Okay. Now, it's time for a decision. After all the sifting and sorting, awareness angling, and preference perusing, it's time to decide *exactly* how you want your life to be different. You're at that point in the shopping experience where you've cruised the store and it's time to make a purchase, only what you're buying now is your *future* and you're purchasing it with your *energy* and *focus*. You're not just window shopping here . . . it's time to *act*. After all the exercises you've done, I'm sure a few specific ideas have come to mind—things you'd like to experience, do, have, or be. You can call them goals or results. You can call them changes or transformations. You can call them affirmations or outcomes. You can call them by a cheesy pet name if you want. It doesn't really matter *what* you call them, because they all mean one thing—intention. Now is the time to make a *decision* about an *intention* (or two . . . or three) that you want to set for yourself.

There are a few steps that will help you define that intention

Mind Movie Example

We are sitting in the gorgeous living room of our new home. It's elegantly decorated—cushy couch, soft leather chairs, beautiful Tuscan tones and artwork, an exquisite area rug, and lovely branches in a huge vase in the corner. The fireplace is lit and we are sitting there chatting, each with a glass of the best red wine in hand. We are happy . . . joyous . . . connected, having an intimate and animated discussion. I can smell the crispness of the fall air, combined with the warmth of the mulberry candle burning in the corner. There's soft piano music playing in the background and everything feels so relaxed and peaceful.

We toast to one another, "To abundance!" he says, and I reply, "To abundance!" The girls run in, breathless from playing. They stop for a quick kiss, and mid-giggle, they shout, "To abundance!" as they scurry off to find yet another adventure. We return to our discussion of gratitude for everything we are so fortunate to be celebrating today, shaking our heads in near-disbelief (the disbelief we *could imagine having* if we weren't living this dream right now). But it's not disbelief . . . just a sense of awe at how amazing our life is today . . . just as we imagined it would be. "We are so blessed," I say. "Truly blessed," he responds.

We recount the journey that brought us to where we are now, with this phenomenal marriage, our healthy minds and bodies and healthy, happy children, work we are passionate about and that makes a difference in people's lives, meaningful pursuits that fill our souls, and a warm, inviting, exquisite home.

We are financially blessed as well, with zero balances on our credit cards and ample cash flow and investments. Our business has grown both in its quality and in its financial rewards, and each year we provide more and more people with the very best services that literally transform their lives. We are creatively meeting the needs of others and enjoying the financial rewards of developing products and services that serve a purpose for those who buy them.

and a few productive tools that will help you stay focused on it. The strategies include That's Affirmative, Vision Boards, and Believing Is Seeing. Be sure to allow yourself some quiet, creative time to work through these exercises, because they are the critical strategies that will create the clarity you need for profound transformation. Your successful use of the LOA in Action depends on your ability to have a rich and detailed picture of your intention, as well as the ready ability to revisit that picture on a moment's notice. And that's what these practices will help you do.

(Your successful use of the LOA in Action depends on your ability to have a rich and detailed picture of your intention, as well as the ready ability to revisit that picture on a moment's notice.)

We are thrilled, too, with our progress in charitable giving that allows us to make a financial investment, in addition to our commitment of our time and talents, to those who can benefit. Our efforts are helping others change their lives and their communities, including children who now have access to resources that help them develop their unique gifts and a pathway to success; women and families who are creating self-sustaining lives; and small community projects that are helping people meet their basic needs so they can build better lives for themselves and their families. We are changing the world through our passions—personal, relationship, and community development, and through our purposeful service to the greater good.

We love our life, we are grateful for all we have, what we have experienced, and what is on its way to us, and we eagerly anticipate the next adventure. We look out the window of that glorious home, toast one more time, and enjoy that beautiful balance between loving where we are and appreciating where we're going. What a blessing and what a joy.

Mind Movie Worksheet

In the space below, record all the ideas, images, and details that come to mind as you produce your Mind Movie.

Life area you are focusing on:

Mind Movie details:

That's Affirmative

Your first step in setting a clear intention is to identify the specific goals or outcomes you want to achieve in a particular area of your life, and then to attach specific language around those goals that make them meaningful, inspiring, and memorable. As you learned earlier, humans are goal-oriented, but I believe that goals sometimes get a bad rap. That's because they are often too general, lacking the detail needed to make them a powerful gravitational force that will pull you toward the outcomes you're seeking. That's why I favor looking at goals from the standpoint of an affirmation, which is in my mind just a very specific way of writing a goal that elicits a feeling of clarity and certainty powered by strong emotions.

Now, affirmations have *also* gotten a bad rap in some circles, which I believe is simply a matter of people not understanding how to craft them. There is a straightforward method that will help you customize affirmations in a way that makes them an indispensable addition to your intention toolkit. At their core, affirmations do four things. First, they *personalize* a goal, making it something truly meaningful to you (not your spouse, your mother, your boss, or the media—but *you*). Second, they infuse your goal with *power*, in the form of emotions and specificity, which makes them more compelling and inspiring. I call this the "spine tingler," because it's any vivid emotion that sends shivers down your spine or gives you goose bumps. These are emotions strong enough to keep you convinced and motivated that this goal is not only possible, but highly—spine-tinglingly—desirable. Third, they bring your goal into the *present tense* (referring to it as though you have already achieved it). This hearkens back to our discussions of neuroscience, where you are literally training the brain to blaze a trail toward the successful accomplishment of your goal. And fourth, they remain *positive*, in that they avoid using "not" or "don't," and focus on what you want rather than what you want to *avoid* (for example, *wealth* rather than being *debt*-free, reaching your *ideal weight* rather than *losing* weight).

Here are a few examples of powerful affirmations:

- "I am elated as I step off the scale at my ideal weight of 130 pounds."

- "I sigh with relief and accomplishment as I drop the last payment in the mail, with all my credit cards paid in full."

- "I am blissfully enjoying an amazing romantic evening with my ideal partner."

- "I feel a sense of profound gratitude and awe as I stand on the lanai of my new home on Keawakapu Beach, Maui."

- "I am thrilled as I walk through the door of my perfectly organized office."

- "I feel overwhelming love and gratitude as I gently cradle my newborn baby in my arms for the first time."

- "I am joyfully looking at my investment balance of $250,000."

- "I feel a sense of total accomplishment and utter pleasure as I look at my planner and see sacred time each and every week devoted to my health and well-being."

- "I triumphantly walk on stage, feeling ecstatic as I accept my promotion to executive director."

- "I give my sister a rowdy high five as we cross the finish line of our first triathlon together."

- "My husband and I toast champagne glasses, giddy with excitement as we look at the financial statements proving we tripled our income this year.

- "I take one last look around and smile as I close the door on the last day of employment here and walk with conviction toward my first day at my dream profession!"

The process of crafting an affirmation is an easy one. First, review your responses from the "You Are Here" and "Sifting Strategies" sections until you identify a specific outcome that you want to enjoy in your life. You are looking for a key goal or change that inspires you—one that you know will make a significant difference in your life. It doesn't have to be a *big* goal or change—just a *meaningful* one. In fact, sometimes it's a good idea to start with something *small* (recall that Kaizen philosophy suggests that small steps lead to big changes over time) to build your skills and your confidence to take on something bigger later on. Next, you go through a simple process of translating that goal or change into an affirmation that inspires you and clearly articulates your intention. It's that easy. Your *That's Affirmative* worksheet takes you step by step through this process.

You are looking for a key goal or change that inspires you—one that you know will make a significant difference in your life. It doesn't have to be a big goal or change— just a meaningful one.

Once you have completed the exercise, I recommend reviewing your affirmations at least once per day for a period of several weeks. This will get you into the habit of focusing on the energy and inspiration behind the affirmation, and will help you commit to memory not only the *goal*, but more importantly, the *feeling* associated with it. And that is by far the most important part of the affirmation process. If you simply read the words of your affirmations or recite them like a grocery list, they'll be just about as powerful as the nutrition information on your cereal box for transforming your life. Informative, perhaps, but hardly inspiring. If, on the other hand, you allow yourself to relax and truly envision every emotional aspect of having already achieved that goal, it becomes this tremendous force that steadily—and easily—draws you toward your goals. So when in doubt, immerse yourself in the emotion of living your dream.

(*When in doubt, immerse yourself in the emotion of living your dream.*)

Vision Boards

Your vision board process builds on several of the exercises you have already completed. It's an extension of your *Shopping Cart* process, where you began collecting images and ideas of your preferences in life, and it springs from the detail you wrote about in both your *I Desire* and your *Mind Movie* exercises. Most important, though, it provides a vivid representation of the affirmation(s) you crafted in your *That's Affirmative* exercise. You create your own personal "vision quest" by creating a vision board (also known as a dream board) for the area of your life you are currently focusing your intention on, and for the affirmation statement(s) you crafted for that realm.

Vision boards are fun, creative processes that allow you to pull together all those images, affirmation statements, quotes, and ideas

That's Affirmative Worksheet

Life area you are focusing on:

1. As you review your responses to the *You Are Here* and *Sifting Strategies* exercises, list the key outcome or goal that you are most interested in focusing on right now. Remember it doesn't have to be *big*, it just needs to *mean something* to you:

2. Review the following characteristics of a good affirmation:

   • *Personal:* It starts with "I," such as "I am," or "I feel."
   • *Powerful:* It integrates specificity—exactly what you want to achieve—with emotion using some type of "feeling" word (elated, blissful, joyful, excited, thrilled, peaceful, grateful).
   • *Present Tense:* It is written as if it is already happening, using an "ing" word or a present-tense verb (I am looking, I step, I am enjoying).
   • *Positive:* It focuses on the outcome you desire, not what you want to change or the process of getting there (avoid words like "not" and "don't want," as well as what you're trying to change). Thus, "debt-free" becomes "wealthy" or "credit cards paid in full" and "weight loss" becomes "ideal weight" or "size 8."

3. Craft a brief, one-sentence, easy-to-recall affirmation for your goal or outcome using the above criteria:

you have been collecting into one global representation of the outcomes you'd like to experience in a particular life area. I have clients who create single vision boards in their three-ring binders, or pull together huge poster boards that take up major wall space. Some use photo albums or bulletin boards or even art frames. One friend makes tiny vision boards on the backs of index cards that contain her affirmations. Whatever method you choose, be sure to attach as many vivid reminders of not only *what* you want, but also *why* you want it, and *how* you will feel experiencing it. Make it as simple or ornate as you want, but just make it.

Then, place your vision board in some strategic location so that you will be sure to see it every day. Ideally, you will review your vision board at the same time that you review your affirmation(s) each day for several weeks. And just like your affirmations, the vision board is only as effective as the *emotion* you put into experiencing in your mind everything you've visually represented on your board. Focus on the feelings associated with *already having those outcomes present in your life*. Center on gratitude, celebration, or any other feeling that will support an emotional high as you look at those images. The goal is to map out your destination in your mind so it will, in turn, create a quicker, more efficient route for you to experience those things in reality. Use the *Vision Board* worksheet to create a framework for your vision board.

> *The goal is to map out your destination in your mind so it will, in turn, create a quicker, more efficient route for you to experience those things in reality.*

Believing Is Seeing

There's a vital element of setting your intention that people tend to overlook, and that's the notion of consciously releasing *limiting* beliefs that have been holding you *back* in life, and replacing them with *empowering* beliefs that move you *forward*. Beliefs are basically meanings we attach to something . . . something we feel certain of, even if we don't have evidence of it. They tell us when to feel pleasure or pain and when we've hit our target or missed it. We need to be very thoughtful about the beliefs we choose because otherwise we wind up working with inaccurate information guiding our choices and coloring our perceptions in life.

> *Beliefs are basically meanings we attach to something . . . something we feel certain of, even if we don't have evidence of it.*

Limiting beliefs are beliefs—often inaccurate and often not consciously chosen—that undermine our ability to do what we want to do in the way we want to do it. Limiting beliefs often belong to several thematic areas, including:

- We aren't *capable* of what we want to do.
- We aren't *worthy* of something (such as love, success, belonging, or joy).

Limiting beliefs look different for everyone and have their origins in childhood, life experience, media messages, and repeated expo-

Vision Board Worksheet

Life area you are focusing on:

If you haven't determined another method you want to use (three-ring binder, photo album, poster board, etc.), use this space to begin creating your vision board. Don't forget to include images, phrases, words, symbols, and certainly your affirmation statements!

sure to others' beliefs. They are the equivalent of "here we go again," where you experience recurring challenges, setbacks, or disappointments in certain areas of your life because these beliefs bring with them ongoing struggle and they serve as roadblocks on your way to success. Examples of limiting beliefs include (but are definitely not limited to!) some of the following statements:

- "Losing weight is hard and I always gain it back."

- "I'm bad at managing money—I always get myself into these messes."

- "You can't make money doing what you love."

- "I always screw up."

- "I don't have enough time to . . . (fill in the blank)."

- "I don't have what it takes to . . . (fill in the blank)."

- "I'm not smart enough."

- "Money doesn't grow on trees; it's hard to get and harder to keep."

- "I can't do anything right."

- "Relationships are hard and unfulfilling."

- "Everyone else is more qualified or skilled than I am; there's no way I can do what they do."

- "It's selfish to want so much . . . (fill in the blank . . . money, success, self-care time, things, opportunity)."

- "I can't ask for help/I'll burden people if I ask for help."

- "All the good mates are taken."

- "My kids will never listen to me."

Empowering beliefs (also referred to as turnaround statements by some LOA practitioners), on the other hand, involve *powerful choices* that move you in the direction you want to go, including:

- "I choose to believe something more productive and to create a different reality."

- "I choose to dispute unproductive thinking and create empowering beliefs."

- "I choose to shape my present and future, not to have others or circumstances shape it for me."

Empowering beliefs share the following characteristics—they:

- Use simple language.

- Are succinct (one sentence).

- Are positive.

- Focus on choice and behavior.

When it comes to addressing your limiting beliefs, your goal is to reprogram them and turn them into empowering beliefs—ones that support your progress and enhance your success. That's where the old saying "seeing is believing" gets an overhaul to become "believing is seeing," since empowering beliefs lead to *results*— real, tangible, and meaningful *results*. The four steps to help you do this are:

1. Identify your limiting belief(s).

2. List the *consequences* of each limiting belief—the negative outcomes, pain, and challenges they create (both in the results you *experience* and in how you *feel*).

3. Transform your limiting belief by creating a powerful, succinct *empowering belief statement* that supports the affirmation(s) you created for this life area.

4. Choose to *adopt this new belief* and live this new reality (it helps to focus on it daily for several weeks).

> *That's where the old saying "seeing is believing"*
> *gets an overhaul to become "believing is seeing,"*
> *since empowering beliefs lead to results—real,*
> *tangible, and meaningful results.*

The following *Believing Is Seeing* example summarizes some limiting beliefs that have been translated into empowering beliefs, and your *Believing Is Seeing* worksheet takes you through these four steps for your priority life area.

You have now worked your way through the action steps for setting your intention. Hopefully this process provided you significant insight into your desires and sufficient inspiration to start manifesting them. Now it's time to translate those results into inspired action, and that's where we're headed in Chapter Seven.

Believing Is Seeing Example

Limiting Belief	Empowering Belief
Losing weight is hard and I always gain it back.	I can lose weight predictably, simply, and long-term. I choose this reality.
I'm bad at managing money—I always get myself into these messes.	I can skillfully manage my money to achieve financial freedom. I choose this reality.
You can't make money doing what you love.	I can love what I do and make a great living doing it. I choose this reality.
Everyone else is more qualified or skilled than I am; there's no way I can do what they do.	I have unique gifts and skills that allow me to achieve success and fulfillment on my own terms. I choose this reality.
I don't have enough time to . . . (keep my office organized, pursue my education, balance work and family).	I have abundant time, energy, and resources to attend to what is most important to me. I choose this reality.

Believing Is Seeing Worksheet

Life area you are focusing on:

1. Identify your limiting belief(s).

   In the past, what has prevented you from getting what you want in this area of your life?

   Review your responses above and create a succinct (one quick sentence) *limiting belief statement*.

2. List the consequences of your limiting belief(s)—the negative outcomes, pain, and challenges they create (both in the results you *experience* and in how you *feel*).

3. Review the characteristics of an empowering belief and then transform your limiting belief by creating a powerful, succinct *empowering belief statement* that supports the affirmation(s) you created for this life area.

   - Simple language
   - Succinct (one sentence)
   - Positive
   - Focuses on choice and behavior

   Your new empowering belief statement:

4. Choose to adopt this new belief and live this new reality. Commit to focusing on it daily for several weeks.

CHAPTER SEVEN

3, 2, 1 Action: Action Steps for Taking Inspired Action

Inspired action, here we come. The process of taking inspired action is at the same time methodical and magical. It's *methodical* in its focus on predictable, consistent steps. It's *magical* in what it yields—results that often far exceed the expectations you had when you set your intentions. Inspired action brings your desires into the realm of day-to-day life, and your dreams into the realm of reality. With that much power at stake, you'd think the process of taking inspired action would be a tough one, but thankfully it's not. Just because it's simple, though, doesn't mean it lacks the ability to transform your life, so don't underestimate its potential.

> *The process of taking inspired action is at the same time methodical and magical.*

In this chapter we'll be covering three action step areas that lead you down the path of inspired action: "Silence!" (quieting your mind), "All About the Ask" (which incorporates three principles—asking simple questions about next steps, taking initiative in the form of immediate action, and gaining momentum with consistent progress), and "Reflect and Revise" (reflecting and building on your progress to sustain continued success). These strategies will help you reframe the concept of that dreaded to-do list into an energizing ta-da! list. Let's dive into the process of how it's done.

Silence!

Quieting your mind is perhaps the most important part of the inspired action equation, because it is from a place of silence and steadiness that your best insights and ideas for forward motion emerge. In his wonderful audio program, *Mindfulness for Beginners*, Jon Kabat-Zinn refers to the idea of meditation (which is just one form of quieting your mind) as a process that helps both calibrate the *instrument* you are using (your mind) to work correctly and create a steady *foundation* for its proper use. He uses the analogy of how difficult it would be to view the moon through a telescope if the telescope were sitting on a water bed. In that case, not only would you be unable to properly calibrate the telescope, but it would be nearly impossible to use it correctly to view your target due to the constant motion of the water bed. Similarly, if your environment is in constant flux, and your mind isn't properly calibrated, how would you possibly be expected to have creative epiphanies about your "next best steps"?

The process of quieting your mind can come from any number of relaxation or meditative processes, including breath work, listening to guided imagery or brainwave-balancing audio programs, yoga and tai chi, or even rhythmic activities that don't require mental focus (such as knitting, crocheting, walking, etc.). "Resources" provides a wide array of suggested books, audios, and websites that can help you explore the right "quieting" process for you, but for the purposes of this chapter, I will refer you back to the meditation exercise "Peace of Mind," discussed in Chapter Five, as one sound technique for quieting the mind. Once you have begun a daily meditative practice, it can become an indispensable tool for creating the silence needed to clearly—and easily—identify your "next best steps." That's when it becomes *all about the ask*.

All About the Ask

After cultivating an appreciation for—and a regular practice of—creating silence in your mind and your life, the core of the entire inspired action strategy is the process of regularly asking yourself, "*What is my next best step?*" It sounds plain, basic, and perhaps almost boring, but it is actually one of the most transformative aspects of the LOA in Action. The very act of "planting the seed" in the form of a question like this causes your mind to begin looking for creative ways to respond. It may not always respond *immediately*, and it may not always respond with something that seems *revolutionary*, but the response—whenever and however it comes—will provide you with important structure for your journey from where you are to where you want to be.

After cultivating an appreciation for—and a regular practice of—creating silence in your mind and your life, the core of the entire inspired action strategy is the process of regularly asking yourself, "What is my next best step?"

Your question is always best posed at the end of a period of silence, as described in the "Silence!" section above. This is when the mind is most receptive to suggestion and most yielding of insight. It's when, like the telescope mentioned above, your mind is calibrated and your environment is steady enough to allow it to perform optimally. Begin by reviewing your affirmation(s) and/or your vision board(s) to remind yourself of the intention(s) you are focused on. Then enjoy that short period of meditation or breath work (depending on the day, your state, and your needs—sometimes a minute or two of deep breathing will get you there, and sometimes a longer period is helpful). At the conclusion of your silence practice, simply ask yourself, "What is my next best step?" Remain in silence until an answer comes or for as long as you feel comfortable, whichever comes first.

If an answer isn't forthcoming, don't push it. Just pose the question again and then go about your daily business. Ask yourself again a few times throughout that day and see whether your mind presents any new insights to you. Usually, it will . . . even if those insights are tiny nudges or seemingly insignificant steps. For instance, sometimes you will get a crisp, clear idea about a critical action you can take, such as, "Submit this proposal to the management team," "Join that new fast fitness center that just opened up," or "Set up automatic payments from my checking account for all of my bills." On the other hand, sometimes you'll think of a resource (like a book, website, person, or organization) that will inform your next inspired action. And sometimes, your mind will simply yield another question for you to ponder, such as, "Why is this so important to me?" or "Who has information that might help me?"

It doesn't matter whether you are moved toward massive action or meaningful baby steps—what matters is that when you get the glimmer of insight, be prepared to record it and act on it *immediately*. Move forward with initiative the moment you get the answer. And just as important . . . take action (no matter how small) every day, since it is *consistency* that builds the *momentum* you will need to enjoy ongoing progress. Meaningful intentions merit consistent action. And remember that small steps can lead to huge changes, so don't count anything out! Your *All About the Ask* worksheet gives you space to record the answers to your questions, as well as to document the consistent steps you took to follow up on those answers.

(*Meaningful intentions merit consistent action.*)

All About the Ask Worksheet

Life area you are focusing on:

Review these quick reminders about the asking and initiative process:

- Review your affirmation(s) and/or your vision board(s) to remind yourself of the intention(s) you are working on.
- Complete a meditation or breath work process to quiet your mind.
- Ask yourself, "What is my next best step?"
- Record your next best step and the details about how you took initiative on that step.

(continued from page 189)

Monday	My Next Best Step:	Initiative/Action I Took:
Tuesday	My Next Best Step:	Initiative/Action I Took:
Wednesday	My Next Best Step:	Initiative/Action I Took:
Thursday	My Next Best Step:	Initiative/Action I Took:
Friday	My Next Best Step:	Initiative/Action I Took:
Saturday	My Next Best Step:	Initiative/Action I Took:
Sunday	My Next Best Step:	Initiative/Action I Took:

Identifying and taking your next best step is one of the most essential aspects of the LOA in Action. But once you do that, it's also important to continually reflect and revise your approach to realizing your dreams.

Reflect and Revise

Reflecting and revising harness that learning mind of yours, allowing it to enrich your approach to manifesting your intention. There
are many ways to reflect on where you've been and revise your
approach to yield even better results, but for me, it always seems to
boil down to three key practices: *Proof of Progress*, the *Two-S
Supercharge*, and *Rhyming Reminders*.

PROOF OF PROGRESS

On the journey toward success and satisfaction in life, there is a
critical practice that many people tend to overlook—a practice so
integral to success that without it, challenges seem more daunting,
progress feels slower, and inspiration tends to wane. It's a practice
that's nearly effortless to implement, which means that it's easy to
underestimate its importance. But it is so powerful in its impact
that it can create a quantum leap in your success in a matter of days
when you make it a daily part of your life. That all-important practice is honoring your own personal *Proof of Progress*.

This strategy is exactly as it sounds . . . the process of cataloging and celebrating evidence of your accomplishments on a regular basis (ideally daily). It's the simple but potent act of reflecting
on your advancement toward your goals and your growth as a
person. This proof of progress, this evidence, can take so many
forms:

- The *small "wins"* that add up to huge triumphs toward your
  larger goals, such as consistency in your daily or weekly health
  habits or learning activities.

- The *changes in thoughts, feelings, or behaviors* that support your progress, such as replacing limiting beliefs with empowering ones, or feeling less stressed and more balanced.

- The *benchmarks* you've hit on the journey toward your ultimate destination, personal or professional, such as making your sales quotas or breaking your caffeine addiction.

- The *serendipitous events* that yielded something significant (a resource, a connection, or a new insight) you have been needing, such as that chance meeting with a life coach or running across a news story on the new business idea you have.

- The *accolades* you've received or feedback you've been given that show you're on track toward your dreams, such as a compliment on your speech at the annual charitable event or a note of thanks from a grateful client or coworker.

- Anything else you can think of that shows proof of progress or evidence of success.

This process should focus both on the tangible and intangible evidence that you're making meaningful progress. The *tangible* evidence includes seeing visible results—things you can clearly observe, from your new pants size to your new bank account balance and from more quality family time to more consistent "me time." Just as important, though, are the *intangible* observations that your life is richer and fuller—how you feel and how you experience the world differently, including your sense of gratitude, balance, self-confidence, or accomplishment.

This process is a matter of being as consistent and methodical about cataloging and celebrating your successes (or evidence of your progress) as you are about mapping out your intentions. Your intentions get you *inspired* and engage you in *action*. Your proof of progress keeps your *commitment* and your *momentum* high by celebrating successes and by providing irrefutable evidence that you are *moving forward* (even when you are struggling or feeling challenged). So take a few moments each day to use the *Proof of Progress* worksheet and watch the magic unfold!

Your intentions get you inspired and engage you in action. Your proof of progress keeps your commitment and your momentum high by celebrating successes and by providing irrefutable evidence that you are moving forward.

Proof of Progress Worksheet

Life area you are focusing on:

On a daily basis, recount your proof of progress toward your intentions. Include both the physical/tangible evidence of growth and success (such as hitting your benchmarks, major steps forward, and new resources or ideas to help you along), as well as the emotional/intangible evidence (such as how you are feeling and major shifts in your attitude or perception). Be as broad as you can in your observations, and as detailed as you can on how and why they matter.

(continued from page 193)

Day	Proof of Progress
Monday	
Tuesday	
Wednesday	
Thursday	
Friday	
Saturday	
Sunday	

Even though you are celebrating progress, it's still a good idea to look for all the ways you can ensure continued advancement toward your intention. That's where the *Two-S Supercharge* comes into play.

THE TWO-S SUPERCHARGE

There are two outstanding ways to supercharge your results, particularly when you are midway through reaching your intention. They are to incorporate *structure* and *support* into your LOA in Action journey.

Structure. When you put structure into place to help you do more of what works and less of what doesn't, it lessens the need for willpower and enhances your chance of incorporating these changes long-term. Structure comes in the form of *habits* and *systems*. You can create structure that helps you attract more of what you want into your life by practicing healthy habits (or replacing unproductive habits with more productive ones) and by setting up systems that improve your chances of building—and maintaining—those healthy habits.

> *When you put structure into place to help you do more of what works and less of what doesn't, it lessens the need for willpower and enhances your chance of incorporating these changes long-term.*

Habits are those things we do (good or bad!) that don't require much conscious thought or energy—they preserve our precious brainpower and physical energy to attend to other (ideally more important!) things. *Healthy* habits, like brushing our teeth and using our seat belts, don't require any willpower and they serve us *well*. *Unhealthy* habits, like negative thinking patterns or eating massive quantities of junk food, also don't require any willpower, but they serve us *poorly*.

Systems are those things that reinforce our ability to build or maintain a habit. So the system that reinforces our toothbrushing habit is the handy placement of a sink, a toothbrush, and toothpaste in the bathroom you frequent, and the system that supports seat belt use is the fact that it's right there when we close the door and a little alarm sounds or a light reminds us to use it. A system that supports the unhealthy habit of negative thinking could be surrounding yourself with negative people, and the system that supports eating junk food could be an endless supply of chips and candy in the pantry.

Your job is to identify which habits and systems will support you in attaining your desires, and then to cultivate them (or to replace unproductive habits and systems with ones that favor success). So what kind of framework can you put into place (or actually practice on a daily basis!)—in the form of habits or systems—that will provide the *structure* you need for success? Does this mean scheduling certain activities into your calendar? Does it mean committing to planning your time every week or every day? Does it mean creating a specific place to get done what you need to do? How about pulling together the tools that make it easy—and pleasurable—to do what you want? Whatever it is, your success will be more likely if you clearly define a new structure (or recommit to an existing one) that will help you move forward with your intention.

For example, say you want to focus on enhancing your marriage because you've found that you are arguing more often and don't seem to take time to connect with one another on a regular basis. You might decide to set up a *structure* in your relationship—and your schedule—that makes "date night" a priority for you. Your new *habit* would be to have an ironclad date night every other week, and your new *system* to support the habit would be to schedule it into both of your calendars, arrange for consistent child care if needed, and agree to take turns every other week making arrangements for your night out.

Or suppose you want to finish your master's thesis, which has been sitting on your desk for the last eighteen months. You may opt to set up a *structure* in your educational process that ensures you will commit the time and attention you need to get it done. Your new *habit* might be to work on your thesis every Tuesday and Thursday from 7 to 9 p.m., and your new *structure* to support that habit might be to create a pleasant, clean place to work on it, to close the door and turn off the phones during that time, and to set a meeting with your thesis advisor every two weeks to help hold you accountable.

The point is that *structure streamlines success*. Save the precious commodities of conscious thought and willpower for what you really want—and need—to spend them on. For everything else, there's a habit and a system to make your life easier.

(*Structure streamlines success.*)

Support. The second S to help keep you on track and turbocharged is the concept of support. This strategy always boils down to "who or what will help ensure that you continue to do what you've set out to do?" Support can come in many forms, including hiring an expert, finding a mentor who's done what you want to do and can show you how to do it, or linking up with an "accountability partner" who can help keep you on track (and you can help him stay the course!). The key is to identify a person or group who will be actively committed to helping you reach your goals by providing great ideas, inspiration, and information, as well as the occasional gentle push in the right direction when your internal nudge-o-meter is faltering. *Whom* can you call on for support, *what specifically* do you need to be supported in and *how* can this person or group best do that?

For instance, if you want to purge your clutter and organize your home, you might gain support from a professional organizer, a super-savvy clutter-free friend, or a book you learned about from the local bookseller. If you want to learn great parenting strategies, you could visit an online community to learn more, or join a local parenting co-op for new ideas and peer support. If you want to start a home-based direct selling business, your options could be taking advantage of company training programs, attending weekly or monthly team meetings, or having regular conversations with your upline to learn their success strategies. Everyone's need—and

The Two-S Supercharge Worksheet

As you reflect on your inspired action, determine where you might integrate more structure or support into your process to help ensure your success.

- *Structure:* Daily habits or systems that will provide a good foundation for progress.
- *Support:* People or groups that serve as "accountability partners" to help you stay committed—and active—doing what you want to do.

	Ideas for Integrating This Concept
Structure	
Support	

preference—for support is unique. The key is to identify the support resources that appeal to you the most and then to weave them into your life in a consistent way. Use your *Two-S Supercharge* worksheet to identify how you can integrate structure and support to supercharge inspired action.

Everyone's need—and preference—for support
is unique. The key is to identify the support resources
that appeal to you the most and then to weave
them into your life in a consistent way.

Once you have created the structure and support system that will help you create optimal outcomes, there are a few strategies that will give you an added boost when you need some extra momentum. These are *rhyming reminders*.

RHYMING REMINDERS

Sometimes, a catchy little phrase can remind you of your opportunities for breaking out of a rut, countering your challenges, or sailing past struggles. These are some of the tools you can use to reflect on your progress and revise your approach as needed. The following three rhyming reminders are meant to give you that glimmer of insight and a dose of resolve just when you need it. They are the *Tweak of the Week, Go with the Flow*, and *Snuggle the Struggle*. When you're feeling challenged about taking inspired action for some reason, tap into one of these options to revise your approach and rebuild your momentum.

Tweak of the Week. Your tweak of the week is the small, seemingly insignificant change you make in your mind-set, your actions, or even your environment to help support your success. It's not uncommon to set out on a journey toward life change and find that your initial great idea isn't yielding optimal results at every turn. That's because we're fortunately learning beings, meant to evolve our ideas and approaches until they produce the outcomes we're after.

(*We're fortunately learning beings, meant to evolve our ideas and approaches until they produce the outcomes we're after.*)

When you want to see better results than you're seeing right now, all you need to identify is one *tiny* adjustment you can make in how you're approaching your goal—one modest modification that might make all the difference. For instance, if you're struggling with making your weekly fitness goal, would it make sense to change the time of day that you work out? Or could you try enlisting a partner to make yourself more accountable? What about selecting a new activity you think might be fun? All these ideas are simple to execute and just might be the key to long-term success. You never know until you try your tweak of the week just how effectively it might move you forward.

Go with the Flow. Periodically we get into the mind-set that when we chart the course for an important goal or outcome in our life, it's supposed to go *exactly* the way we envisioned, according to the *precise* time line we imagined. Since this is almost *never* the case for a variety of reasons, it's a good idea to learn to go with the flow when it will serve you. What this means is that, so long as you are moving forward and making progress toward what you desire, the route doesn't need to conform to a *mental map* as much as you need to be able to follow your *internal compass*. Just as a stream finds a gentle route around rocks in its path, you, too, can learn to go with the flow. When you relax into your journey, you might be amazed at the quality—and the productivity—of a few little twists and turns in your trip. Stay focused on the end result you're after, use that internal compass often, and know that you can navigate around the occasional obstruction with ease and simplicity.

For example, I had a client who applied for several different positions in her company because she was ready for a new challenge. Though she was a stellar employee, she was turned down on each occasion for various reasons. She chose to remain upbeat because she felt certain that if she kept her focus on what she *really* wanted (the *ideal* new role that matched her passion and her skills), the right opportunity would present itself at the perfect time. Because she didn't allow herself to become jaded and riddled with disappointment, she was able to realize that the problem was that this *company* was not her ideal company, so how could her ideal *role* be there? She opened herself up to other options and within a month was hired at her ideal company in her ideal role. All because she chose to go with the flow.

> *So long as you are moving forward and making progress toward what you desire, the route doesn't need to conform to a mental map as much as you need to be able to follow your internal compass.*

Snuggle the Struggle. Sometimes you get to that point in your change process—and most of us do!—when it seems like everything's a struggle. Nothing feels simple, and frustration tends to get the better of you. This is your alarm clock telling you to step back, analyze your situation, and use a softer, gentler approach. It's kind of like one of your parenting options when your toddler (or heck, your teenager for that matter) borders on full-scale meltdown. There's sometimes that amazing moment when you can transform the entire outcome simply by stepping in to offer a hug and a moment of TLC. Often, what humans need in a moment of utter frustration is just a bit of *nurturing*, a moment of *calm*, a shot of *self-care* to cure what ails us. That's when you can choose to snuggle the struggle. When you find yourself banging your head against the wall, or you feel like your intentions are butting up against every obstacle known to man, this is usually a sign that you need to pull back and regroup. You're trying *too* hard and suffering *too* much to achieve this noble thing in your life. Stop right there, take a deep breath, and take a moment or two (or three!) to *snuggle the struggle*. When you find yourself feeling that sense of overwhelming frustration or pure anxiety about why it's not working out as you planned, identify something you can do *right now* to take care of yourself. Take a walk or take a nap. Get a shoulder rub or hug your favorite animal. Soak up some sun or soak in a hot bath. Call a friend or call on your spiritual side. Whatever it is, divert your attention from the struggle to the snuggle—self-care will give you enough respite to return with a clear mind and fresh perspective.

> *Often, what humans need in a moment of utter frustration is just a bit of nurturing, a moment of calm, a shot of self-care to cure what ails us.*

Consider using the *Rhyming Reminders* worksheet to identify some creative ways that you might revise your approach to taking inspired action toward your intention.

Rhyming Reminders Worksheet

As you reflect on your progress toward your intention, consider applying one or all of the Rhyming Reminder strategies to your situation when you need it.

- *Tweak of the Week:* One small change you can make to enhance your experience or improve your results.
- *Go with the Flow:* A way to gently navigate around something in your path rather than straining against it.
- *Snuggle the Struggle:* A moment or an act of self-care that gives you respite from your journey so that you can return to it with a clear mind and a fresh perspective.

First, identify the challenge you're facing, and then note which of the rhyming reminders you used and the impact it had on either how you felt or your progress . . . or both.

Challenge	Outcome of Using Rhyming Reminders

You now have an outstanding array of tools for taking inspired action that supports your intention. Keep focusing your energy on a daily basis to hone the creativity and momentum it takes to realize your dreams. You will be astounded at the progress you can make by taking one small step each day—your next best step—toward your intention.

Your Second Step

I'll admit, I was going to say some pithy version of, "Now it's time for you to take your first step," when I realized that you've already done that—you picked up this book and you've read it. That was your first step. Now, it's time to take your *second* step . . . to take *action* on what you've learned here. Throughout this book, you have been introduced to the principles of *why* the LOA works and *how* you can make it work for you using the LOA in Action model (Choose Your State, Set Your Intention, and Take Inspired Action). You have explored a wide array of strategies for developing your own LOA in Action plan. And you've seen some examples of how others have harnessed the power of the LOA to purposefully design their life experience. You now have the information and the inspiration, the principles and the practices you need to move forward, but that's just the beginning.

Remember that your second step can be any positive, purposeful strategy that helps you draw more of what you want into your life (and less of what you don't want). The key is to take thoughtful action. That's why this book isn't called *The Law of Attraction in Review* . . . or *in Theory* . . . or *in Concept*. It's called *The Law of Attraction in Action*. In the words of Václav Havel, "Vision is not enough, it must be combined with venture. It is not enough to stare up the steps, we must step up the stairs." So what will it be? It's time to choose your state, set your intention, and take that next best step to put the LOA in Action in your life. Best wishes on your journey!

RESOURCES

Videos

The Secret
What the Bleep Do We Know?

Books

Assaraf, John, *Having It All*
Begley, Sharon, *Train Your Mind, Change Your Brain*
Benson, Herbert, *The Breakout Principle*
Benson, Herbert, *The Relaxation Response*
Braden, Gregg, *The Divine Matrix*
Byrne, Rhonda, *The Secret*
Byrne, Rhonda, *The Secret Gratitude Book*
Canfield, Jack, *Jack Canfield's Key to Living the Law of Attraction*
Canfield, Jack, *The Success Principles*
Chasse, Betsy, *The Little Book of Bleeps*
Chopra, Deepak, *The Seven Spiritual Laws of Success*
Chopra, Deepak, *The Spontaneous Fulfillment of Desire*
Csikmenthalyi, Mihaly, *Finding Flow*
Davis, Deanna, *Living With Intention*
Davis, Deanna, and Jen White, *Manifest This!*
Demartini, John, *Count Your Blessings*
Demartini, John, *The Gratitude Effect*
Doyle, Bob, *Wealth Beyond Reason*

Resources

Dwoskin, Hale, *The Sedona Method*

Dyer, Wayne, *Inspiration—Your Highest Calling*

Dyer, Wayne, *The Power of Intention*

Emoto, Masuro, *The Hidden Messages in Water*

Forster, Sandy, *How to Be Wildly Wealthy Fast*

Hawkins, David, *Power-vs-Force*

Hicks, Esther, *The Amazing Power of Deliberate Intent*

Hicks, Esther, *Ask and It Is Given*

Hicks, Esther, *The Astonishing Power of Emotions*

Hicks, Esther, *The Law of Attraction*

Hill, Napoleon, *Think and Grow Rich*

Kabat-Zinn, Jon, *Full Catastrophe Living*

Kabat-Zinn, Jon, *Wherever You Go, There You Are*

Lipton, Bruce, *The Biology of Belief*

Look, Carol, *Attracting Abundance with EFT—Emotional Freedom Technique*

Losier, Michael, *Law of Attraction*

Maurer, Robert, *The Kaizen Way*

McColl, Peggy, *Your Destiny Switch*

McTaggart, Lynne, *The Intention Experiment*

Pert, Candace, *Molecules of Emotion*

Proctor, Bob, *You Were Born Rich*

Radmacher, Mary Anne, *Lean Forward Into Your Life*

Ray, James, *The Science of Success*

Robbins, Anthony, *Unlimited Power*

Seligman, Martin, *Authentic Happiness*

Seligman, Martin, *Learned Optimism*

Shimoff, Marci, *Happy for No Reason*

Taylor, Sandra Anne, *Quantum Success*

Vitale, Joe, *The Attractor Factor*

Vitale, Joe, *The Key*

Wattles, Wallace, *The Science of Getting Rich*

Weider, Marcia, *Dreams Are Whispers from the Soul*
Weider, Marcia, *Making Your Dreams Come True*

Audios

Holosync (brain sync audio for meditation), www.centerpointe.com
Kabat-Zinn, Jon, *Guided Mindfulness Meditation*
Kabat-Zinn, Jon, *Mindfulness for Beginners*
Metamusic (brain sync audio for meditation, sleep, creativity, etc.),
    www.hemi-sync.com

Websites

Abraham-Hicks Publications, www.abraham-hicks.com
Applied Insight, www.appliedinsight.net
Authentic Happiness, www.authentichappiness.sas.upenn.edu
Deanna Davis, www.deannadavis.net
Dream University, www.dreamcoach.com
The Gratitude Diet, www.gratitudediet.com
Heart Math, www.heartmath.org
Ingrid Agnew, www.ingridagnew.com
Jack Canfield, www.jackcanfield.com
Mary Anne Radmacher, www.maryanneradmacher.com
Reflective Happiness, www.reflectivehappiness.com
The Secret, www.thesecret.tv
The Sedona Method, www.sedona.com
Steve Pavlina, www.stevepavlina.com
TUT's Adventurers Club, www.tut.com
Wealth Beyond Reason, www.wealthbeyondreason.com
World Center for Emotional Freedom Technique (EFT), www.emofree.com

Music—Inspirational

"Anyway" (Martina McBride)
"All the Good" (Jana Stanfield)
"Amazing Things" (Jana Stanfield)
"Breakaway" (Kelly Clarkson)
"Circle of Life" (Elton John)
"Coming Out of the Dark" (Gloria Estefan)
"Conviction of the Heart" (Kenny Loggins)
"Don't Stop" (Fleetwood Mac)
"Give a Little Bit" (Supertramp)
"Good Riddance" (Green Day)
"Hands" (Jewel)
"I Hope You Dance" (Lee Ann Womack)
"If I Were Brave" (Jana Stanfield)
"Live Like You Were Dying" (Tim McGraw)
"More Than Enough" (Jana Stanfield)
"My Next 30 Years" (Tim McGraw)
"My Wish" (Rascal Flatts)
"Ordinary Miracle" (Sarah McLachlan)
"The Hand That Gives the Rose" (Coles Whalen)
"These Are Days" (10,000 Maniacs)

Music—Energizing

"Any Way You Want It" (Journey)
"Baby, I'm a Star" (Prince)
"Celebration" (Kool & The Gang)
"Dare to Be" (Jana Stanfield)
"Don't Stop Thinking About Tomorrow" (Fleetwood Mac)

"Feels Good" (Tony, Toni, Toné)

"Flashdance/What a Feeling" (Irene Cara)

"FunkyTown" (PseudoEcho)

"Get on Your Feet" (Gloria Estefan)

"Gonna Make You Sweat/Everybody Dance Now" (C&C Music Factory)

"Good Vibrations" (The Beach Boys)

"Hips Don't Lie" (Shakira)

"I'm a Believer" (Smashmouth)

"It's My Life" (Bon Jovi)

"Jump" (Van Halen)

"Let the Change Begin" (Jana Stanfield)

"Let's Go Crazy" (Prince)

"Life Is a Highway" (Rascal Flatts)

"Life Will Never Be the Same" (Haddaway)

"Lovin' Every Minute of It" (Loverboy)

"Mony Mony" (Billy Idol)

"Pump up the Jam" (Technotronic)

"ROCK in the USA" (John Cougar Mellencamp)

"Simply the Best" (Tina Turner)

"Top of the World" (Van Halen)

"Unbelievable" (Diamond Rio)

"Unbelievable" (EMF)

"Walking on Sunshine" (Katrina and the Waves)

"We Got the Beat" (Go-Go's)

"We Will Rock You" (Queen)

"What I Like About You" (The Romantics)

"What Is Love" (Haddaway)

"Whenever, Wherever" (Shakira)

"You Spin Me Round" (Dead or Alive)

ABOUT THE AUTHOR

Photo by Diane Maehl

Deanna Davis, PhD, is the author of *The Law of Attraction in Action*, *Manifest This!*, and the bestselling *Living With Intention*. After building a thriving practice as a life and business coach, Deanna turned her efforts toward her roles as an author and professional speaker. Through those activities, she helps her readers and audiences transform their minds, their actions, and their lives.

As a speaker and trainer, Deanna has helped audiences master topics such as Success Strategies, Creating a Powerful Perspective, Peak Performance in Work and Life, and the Law of Attraction. She has served companies including Farmers Insurance, the National Management Association, Pacific Gas and Electric Transmission, Sensaria Natural Bodycare, the Interagency Committee of State Employed Women, and *Northwest Woman* magazine, among others. She also provides a series of workshops, seminars, retreats, and programs on topics such as *The Law of Attraction in Action*, *Living With Intention*, *Your Ideal Weight*, *Success in Seven*, and *Marriage Essentials*.

Known for her energetic and upbeat nature, Deanna's style offers a delicious blend of humor, practical information, inspiration, and motivation. She combines scientifically proven principles with practical strategies that help people enhance their quality of life and their level of success. She integrates into all of her work cutting-edge research from the arenas of Positive

Psychology, peak performance, neuroscience, and mind/body health, and expertly balances those foundations by providing readers and audiences the inspiration to try something new and the confidence to implement it.

For immediate access to an array of free resources (including e-books, audios, and newsletters), visit Deanna online at www.deannadavis.net.

To inquire about Deanna's availability as a speaker or trainer, please contact her office at:

Applied Insight, LLC

509.532.1600 or 877.958.1600

www.deannadavis.net or www.appliedinsight.net